Selfhood and U.S. Democracy

Edith E. Muesing-Ellwood

Plain View Press
P.O. 42255
Austin, TX 78704

plainviewpress.net
sb@plainviewpress.net
512-441-2452

Copyright © 2010 Edith E. Muesing-Ellwood. All rights reserved under International and Pan-American Copyright Conventions. No part of this book may be reproduced or distributed in any form or by any means, or stored in a data base or retrieval system, without written permission from the author. All rights, including electronic, are reserved by the author and her publisher.

ISBN: 978-1-935514-57-2
Library of Congress Number: 2010932955

Cover art: Myke Maldonado.
Cover design by Susan Bright.

To Danny

Contents

Preface	7
Introduction	9
Chapter One The Establishment of United States Democracy	17
Chapter Two Mass Culture and Democracy	23
Chapter Three The Mass Media	35
Chapter Four The Internet	43
Chapter Five Selfhood	61
Chapter Six Exercising Values	73
Conclusion Where We Go Now	87
Epilogue	95
Notes	97
Glossary	100
Resources	101
About the Author	109

Preface

I have written Selfhood and U.S. Democracy not because the topic of U.S. democracy has not been discussed enough, but because I believe the roots of democracy and its values derive themselves from the goodness underlying the unconscious framework of each individual. This issue is worth discussing because, among other reasons, the United States is a nation of individuals. While many scholars and authors have discussed the mass culture threatening United States democracy, I offer an answer to its malfunction through a negation (refutation) of it and a return to individual selfhood and love.

In Selfhood and U.S. Democracy I focus on the principles of democracy as originally found in the Declaration of Independence and the U.S. Constitution, based upon freedom, equality, and justice. Each person has the right to pursue happiness as he or she defines it personally within the collective whole of society.

I have not dealt with the technological miracles of our post-modern times because they speak for themselves. But, success has brought problems with it. What I have attempted to do is tackle some fundamental issues in regard to the individual and our democratic system. I delve into the alienation, anomie, and accompanying depression, which many individuals suffer due to mass culture. I point out some of the disillusionment individuals feel in regard to the functioning of our political and governmental systems. Through an examination of principles associated with the concept of selfhood, I believe I have found an alternative to the individual's objectification and loss of self-esteem today.

I conclude on a positive note concerning the future of U. S. democracy. Reform is possible on the part of subject individuals interpreting values on a personal basis within the transcendental spiritual relationship that gives the interpretation a foundation of perfection. This leads to societal and political action since we are all part of the greater whole.

I am not new to the topics discussed in this book. I have written a number of articles and two books concerning mass culture and United States democracy since beginning my research in the 1980s. I feel that never before have my ideas been more relevant. Our times pose a dire need for them to be discussed – not because there is anything wrong with technology – but because of the way many people in society utilize it and because of the political road we have taken.

I would like to add that time and progress require a reinterpretation of the humanitarian values of freedom and equality as originally presented by the Founding Fathers and that through a reinterpretation of our concept of democracy these values can go further than first established by our *Declaration of Independence* and the *U.S. Constitution*.

In closing, I would like to encourage readers to consult the original sources I have presented and discussed in this book; for example, the works of C.G. Jung and Mortimer Adler. Reference to their sources can be found in the bibliography at the end of *Selfhood and U.S. Democracy*.

>
> Edith E. Muesing-Ellwood
> February 2010

Introduction

I

In a democracy the individual self is granted the freedom to pursue his or her own happiness as long as it does not infringe upon the rights of others. In theory all government decision-making is based upon the consent of free and equal citizens functioning in the collective of our nation state, the United States of America. This depends upon the nature of the unconscious in each individual, which ensures the possibility of self-development based upon free will as long as the freedom and rights of others are not infringed upon.

The eminent psychoanalyst, C.G. Jung, describes how the individual can strive toward goodness in determining his or her selfhood. This goodness is necessary for democracy to flourish as a unit of competing and conflicting individuals. Jung defines the "self" as the organizing principle of personality that gives it its oneness or unity. When we ask ourselves "Who am I?" we identify ourselves in terms of selfhood.

According to Jung, the inherent unconscious drive for human unity exists through the collective unconscious. Together with the personal unconscious, the root of individual subject being, it results in the thought, will, and the self-realization of the individual. Our government must protect this essential development, which can be termed a "becoming" process.

Because of the unifying nature of the collective unconscious, an association develops among individuals that allows for social cohesion even in times of critical evaluation and change, both in regard to individual self-development and in terms of reforming a democracy when practice no longer reflects democratic ideals. The individual is capable of love of himself or herself and of humanity. Values retain an absolute nature through a participation in the transcendental relationship with the Spiritual.

The right to happiness is defined by each individual's own selfhood. Democracy flourishes even with each individual having his or her own selfish interests because of the common ground of ancestry in the collective unconscious as described by Jung. The values of freedom and equality are protected by the laws of the land in the United States of America. This umbrella has encompassed more and more people as our democracy has progressed both in theory and in practice.

It should be noted that equality has not always been applied to everyone in our land. For example, Congress did not even prohibit the importation of slaves until 1807, and slavery was not ended until the Civil War. Today we have an African-American as President. Also, women were not granted the right to vote until the Nineteenth Amendment became law in 1920. Today we have equal work / equal pay laws. The fundamental values of freedom, equality, and justice have expanded over time.

Selfhood and U.S. Democracy discusses mass-consumption culture, which grew in the 1950s, and was later accompanied by computer age technology. It has resulted in psychological problems across social and economic lines. Personal freedom has been lost to the process of mass consumption as those in control of production and advertising determine our socio-economic system with superimposed desires falsely termed "needs." Is it really necessary to buy a new car just because a neighbor has or to succeed just for the purpose of succeeding with no goal in mind?

Returning self-control to the individual and democratic power to the people is a major issue in the United States today. Not only does the individual lose control of him – or herself, but also the interaction in society becomes irrational. The whole is equal to the sum of its parts.

Through an examination of the principles associated with the concept of selfhood, I believe I have found an alternative to the individual's objectification and loss of inner self-esteem. I develop a positive attitude on the future of United States democracy, based on the action of individuals exerting their self-love and their respect for the rest of society.

II

The structural/functionalism of the democratic political process changes demands (input) into public policy (output). The public, as individual citizens, and as individuals represented in formal, or informal interest groups or subcultures that are not wanton crowds, articulates and aggregates wants in a communication process that exerts pressure on the policy-making apparatus of government. This is how laws change. Government either legislates and executes policy to meet these demands or adjudicates change according to the existing laws of the nation state.

There are two forms of democracy: direct rule by the people or, as in the United States, rule through a representative system in which each individual exerts free will to elect those who will represent him or her in policy decision-making. The majority rules in the United States through laws, which citizens obey through a collective will, be it active or passive.

Theoretically, a free subject takes into account personal and collective needs in light of a potential for constructive development. In our democracy active political role-playing by citizens sets a precedent for subsequent decisions made. This is how civil rights laws were enacted over time in the name of progress.

If free to reflect, the human psyche is active rather than passive and capable of arriving at independent decisions in terms of self-interest and adaptation to society. The key point here is that between ideas and overt acts there is a state of reflection, a state in which the individual decides what to do. Once an individual in society achieves an awareness of himself or herself as a political actor, he or she is capable of exerting pressure for change.

In theory, in the United States democracy, along with granting such fundamental freedoms as speech, press, religion and assembly, calls on the individual to act with self-restraint to protect the freedom of each and all other citizens. Civil liberties are protected by the Constitution and other laws so that no one group or individual has the political power to curtail the rights of others. Our democracy balances and separates the powers of the president, the judiciary, and the legislature on the federal, state, and local levels so that absolute power by a person or group of people is prevented.

In theory, democracy is realized when individual subject beings interact in society to influence the outcome of government policies for all through a structure that is accessible to all. This is presupposed on the fact that individuals act in a common rational manner under similar conditions.

This supposition puts constraints on the concept that the individual acts as an isolated subject being to essentially develop him- or herself according to free will regardless of others. While the institutions of nations may not function exactly like the citizens composing them, as part of the collective, individuals interact with each other to produce change in the input and output of government policy without causing strife.

In this book I present Jung's theory that the unconscious is composed of the personal and the collective, thus the existential position that consciousness is void has no merit as long as the collective nature is considered to be real and composed of archetypes or patterns that bind us to each other and to all individuals of the past.

I do make some references to existentialists in that their merit lies in the development of the theory of subject individuals, which is comparable to Jung's theory of the personal unconscious. The existentialists make a distinction between the individual as subject and as an object that is manipulated today in mass-consumption culture or rather between the thinking person and the one who leaves answers up to the crowd.

In our democracy, it is apparent that the unifying nature of the collective unconscious allows for social cohesion even in times of critical evaluation, change, and the general functioning of the individual subject's will. The awareness of a free subject takes into account individual and collective needs in light of a potential for constructive development. In a democracy, active political role-playing by citizens sets a precedent for subsequent decisions made politically.

The ethics underlying the theory and practice of a democracy is based upon the affirmation of human self-love found in the transcendental participation with Absolute

Love. This absoluteness gives a person confidence in his or her values. Reason is a mode of thought and action that along with love toward others upholds democracy and defies oppression.

Self-determination for the individual is real as long as the citizenry is composed of rational and ethical people free from manipulation through propaganda. To the extent that today's civil society is rational and free, it is capable of sustaining a democracy. To the extent that it believes propaganda, it is crippled. Self-love and love of one's country can work with ethics and reason to ensure that democracy functions according to its established principles.

The more competent an individual sees him- or herself to be politically, the more active he or she will become. As citizens see policy output reflect their demands, they will more willingly participate as individuals, members of formal organizations, and/or as part of informal face-to-face groups composed of individuals.

United States democracy requires that individuals acting together as a nation ensure the legitimacy of the government. It assumes that citizens have the choice to reform the political and governmental system. Democracy is not only given to the people by the laws of the nation state and the norms of society but, ultimately, by the self-love of each individual in developing his or her own essential nature.

The pervasiveness of the mass-consumption culture today requires a reexamination of the principles of liberty, equality, and justice to determine how far American society has digressed from functioning according to the true meaning of these principles. Through a dialectical negation (or refutation using reason) of the falsehood found today this would allow

United States citizens and their elected officials to reaffirm democracy's principles to reality for the purpose of reestablishing an ethical system.

Today, in the face of the complexities of modern life, many individuals in society suffer from identity crises. While peasant village dwellers were given a secure place in society by birth and knew what was expected of them, individuals in today's mobile technological society are left alone to determine their identity in an impersonal world. The problems of alienation and anomie, along with depression, must be overcome through a dialectical awakening based upon self-love and a belief in the goodness of one's fellow citizens.

This makes a democracy dependent upon the decisions of individuals difficult to secure, yet it must secure this decision-making. Super-imposed consumption pleasures and buying for the sake of buying do not bring happiness and must be eradicated. The individual must be in total connection with his or her inner self for democracy to flourish according to its founding principles.

Compassion and love are fundamental to relations between human beings.

– The Dali Lama

Acknowledgments

To begin with let me say that I made an exhaustive effort to find all people having any rights or interests in the quotes appearing in this book and tried to obtain permission from them to use such quotes. If oversights have occurred, it was by accident on my part, and I request forgiveness from those so injured.

I would like to thank the American Political Science Association for its excellent research material and the librarians at East Stroudsburg University Kemp Library who helped me in my research endeavors. Also, may I express my gratitude to Yale Professor Emeritus Louis Dupré for his kind and thoughtful praise concerning my work.

I would also like to thank Sharon Napolitano whose formatting and annotating skills were invaluable. Among the other people to be thanked are Denise Robbins and Judy Bush of Eagle Valley Printing in East Stroudsburg, PA for accommodating me in Xeroxing and collating duties.

Many thanks go to Helen Vitoria and Margaret Buser for taking time from their busy schedules to endorse my book and especially to Myke Maldonado for his artistic skills in creating and producing my book cover design.

Special thanks go to my children, Jeanie, Colin, and Caroline Ellwood, and to Amanda Smith and Sean Peschel for their encouragement and support. In particular, I would like to thank my husband, William (Danny) Ellwood PE, whose criticism and compassion made this book possible.

Lastly but certainly not least, I would like to thank Susan Bright, who as publisher, is responsible for turning *Selfhood And U.S. Democracy* from a manuscript into the book it now is.

Edith E. Muesing Ellwood

Chapter One
The Establishment of United States Democracy

I

United States democracy was established to protect the individual's rights within the context of the common good. It takes into consideration both economic and political rights because "happiness" depends upon both. The laws of this nation incorporate the ideals of liberty and equality for the purpose of achieving a just and viable political community.

The individual's right to pursue his or her own happiness is protected as long as he or she does not infringe upon the rights of others. The republican form of government established in the United States is based upon a public trust or contract between the public and the government of officials elected to govern by representing the public will through majority rule.

The *Declaration of Independence of the United States of America* was adopted on July 4, 1776. It defines democracy according to the following principles:

> "We hold these truths to be self-evident, that all men are created equal; that they are endowed by their Creator with certain inalienable rights; that among these are life, liberty, and the pursuit of happiness. That to secure these rights, governments are instituted among men, deriving their just powers from the consent of the governed; that whenever any form of government becomes destructive of these ends, it is right of the people to alter or to abolish it, and to institute a new government, laying its foundation on such principles, and organizing its powers in such form, as to them shall seem most likely to effect their safety and happiness…"[1]

The *Declaration of Independence* served the colonists' purpose of establishing their separation from the British Crown. Its principles along with the Constitution and the Bill of Rights became the foundation of United States democratic ideology. The values of freedom, equality, and justice legitimized the United States government and laws. They were derived partly from the philosophy of John Locke, as expressed in his work *Of Civil Government: The Second Treatise*, written in 1690.

Locke stated in his treatise that all men prior to entering society are free and equal in their natural environment. He went on to say that the laws of nature governing the state of nature come from God and are discovered by reason. Locke held that the fundamental rights belonging to the individual are life, liberty, and property. These rights were incorporated into the *Declaration of Independence* by Thomas Jefferson, who substituted the word "happiness" for "property." The substitution suggests that laboring on one's property for one's own advantage results in personal happiness. Thus, as used here, the terms of property and happiness are interchangeable even though today the definition of happiness has expanded to include general contentment and well-being.

According to Locke, governments are established by a social contract of unanimous popular consent in order to protect the fundamental rights of each individual entering society.

Once a government is established, all members of society must submit to the will of the majority according to the understanding that the primary function of government is to protect each individual from the infringement of his or her rights by another, regardless of who constitutes the majority at any particular time.

Locke added that should the government fail to protect society, it is the right of the people to abolish it in favor of a new government that adheres to the social contract. The government is to be entrusted with enough power to protect the economic pursuits of the populace. Herein lies the implied connection between the principles of democracy and free enterprise that has existed since the United States first became a nation with some restrictions imposed as time went on.

The colonists had rejected the British monarchy with its sacredness of tradition and aristocratic privileges. They wanted freedom from the British Crown, which had refused them political representation and taxed them without their consent. Their government was to be based upon the right to political self-determination. Associated with this was the right to the product of one's labor. These rights were to be protected by the government and the political process.

Effective March 4, 1789, the Founding Fathers established the framework for their government in the *Constitution of the United States*, a social contract stipulating that the power of government is derived from popular consent. It begins as follows:

> "We the people of the United States, in order to form a more perfect union, establish justice, insure domestic tranquility, provide for the common defense, promote the general welfare, and secure the blessings of liberty to ourselves and our posterity, do ordain and establish this *Constitution for the United States of America.*"[2]

The *Constitution* (along with the *Bill of Rights*, further amendments, and the laws on the national, state and local levels) conforms to the principles expressed in the *Declaration of Independence*. Gradually, they were expanded to include those who were originally excluded in practice.

The system of government proposed ensures a separation of powers among the branches of government, as well as a system of governmental "checks and balances" to safeguard the populace from any form of government tyranny. It was decided that the government should be limited in power because Americans did not trust power. Government was instituted by the people to be ruled by representatives accepting a popular mandate to govern according to law and the will of the majority.

Alexis de Tocqueville, visiting the United States in the early 1800s, noted the following in regard to the attachment men felt to the country. In addition to an instinctive patriotism there was a more enduring one. De Tocqueville wrote the following:

> "It springs from knowledge; it is nurtured by the laws; it grows by the exercise of civil rights; and in the end, it is confounded with the personal interests of the citizen. A man comprehends the influence, which the well-being of his country has upon his own; he is aware that the laws permit him to contribute to that prosperity, and he labors to promote it."[3]

The democratic rights of liberty, equality, and the pursuit of happiness expressed in the *Declaration of Independence* and protected by *The Constitution* and subsequent interpretations by the Supreme Court provide the United States government with the legitimacy it requires to function – that is, justice by law not only in the interest of society as a whole but also of each individual in society.

Samuel P. Huntington, in his book, *American Politics: The Promise of Disharmony*, points out that there have been periods of "creedal passion" or moral awakening in American history. The Revolutionary War was the first such crisis. The thought process that led to the war was dialectical in nature. Americans were guided by the principles they set forth in the Declaration of Independence to establish a governmental system granting them a voice over their own affairs and control over their own property and output of their labor. This amounted to a negation of the subjugation they had suffered under British rule, which Americans treated as their antithesis to be negated or rejected.

During the periods of American history, democracy provided the moral impetus needed for reform. The American Revolution, the Jacksonian Era, the Progressive Era, and the decades of the 1960s and 1970s, resulted from a blatant disregard of ethical democracy through an excessive use of power. They were the result of a "consciousness crisis" on the part of segments of society. The periods achieved reform according to the ethical principles democracy represents while at the same time maintaining society as a cohesive unit that endured the conflicts associated with social, political, and/or economic change. Government continued to function without interruption during and after the enactment of reforms, but its functioning reflected the changes in policy as reform was instituted.

II

By its critical nature, democracy as ideology is an art form. Art is detached from reality, as are values from their pragmatic interpretation. Through the application of values to reality it is possible to point out the weaknesses and failures of society in action. However, unlike art, which does not leave the sublime, the democratic values of liberty, equality, and justice leave it to attempt an approximation of the ideal in the real.

If individuals in society possess active free wills, they can combine an awareness of the contradiction between democracy as an ideal and the reality of its practice to bring about a positive synthesis of the two through subsequent action on their part. The Revolutionary War and other periods of awakening in American history exhibit such change.

Jerome Armstrong and Markos Moulitsas Zuniga point out in their book, *Crashing the Gate*, that through a combination of grassroots and computer "netroots," the people of the United States are now undertaking a movement to return politics to the people. This can be termed our period of creedal passion.

Each person's awareness of being not only a self but also a self among others in society's collective, allows the individual to make decisions for the general good through the protection of the inalienable rights not only for him- or herself, but also for other members of society. In the United States these decisions take into consideration the objective social, economic, and political needs of each member of society within the context of established laws and accepted practices. They become collective decisions through the individual participating in elections and through participation in informal and formal interest groups through which pressure is exerted toward government officeholders to make and enforce laws for the benefit of the individual and society as a whole as well as its environment.

Reform is possible if it is instituted by an awakening of consciousness because, contrary to Marxist theory, consciousness is not inferior to socio-economic conditions, nor is it part of nature, and ideology need not be determined by the economic production system of a nation. If consciousness is free, it can determine what "ought to be" in light of reality's contradiction to it. The rational and ethical possibilities form the pragmatic framework for action to produce change toward a new "synthesis" of the ideal and the real. Reform brings political, social, and economic relations into a closer harmony with ethical values.

United States democracy leads to action for reform because it serves to remind individuals of its ethical and rational goals in light of specific grievances. It leads to action based upon a general aim that takes into consideration past experience with reform or the negation of previous deviation from the true principles of our democracy for understanding the current situation and future implications of a new action to be taken.

Unfortunately, when ideological references are needed to instill unity and allegiance, there is often a deliberate and irrational distortion of principles for that purpose. In such cases, United States democracy serves much the same purpose of former Soviet communist propaganda to achieve public support for maintaining and protecting the goals of those in power by a manipulation of the individual's perception of reality making each person part of an object mass or crowd.

For example, President George W. Bush's oratory in support of the Iraq War to protect the United States and spread democracy after the terrorist attacks in 2001 on the World Trade Center in New York and the Pentagon in Washington, D.C., was found later not to be in support of the facts that there was no nuclear arsenal in Saddam Hussein's Iraq and no weapons of mass destruction.

President Bush gained public support for destroying what he called the "axis of evil" in the Middle East in his 2002 State of the Union Address. His statements were made without adequate verification. This does not prove that only misperceptions caused support of the war. Yet, they were a key factor in rallying the public around the President, at the time the United States was most vulnerable by being attacked on its own soil by irrational and immoral terrorists.

In the past blatant disregard of ethical democracy through an excessive use of power resulted in a "consciousness crisis" on the part of the American people and change toward a more ethical democracy. The bond formed on the basis of the values of freedom and equality held the society and its government together without interruption during and after the enactment of the reforms. Because they could so function, the changes in policy could be instituted.

Such a consciousness crisis is needed today as witnessed by the 2008 presidential election of Barack Obama who promised the public change. A negation of the irrationality of today's culture is required to create a new culture that meets the goals of rational individuals with active free wills attempting pragmatic solutions to social, political and economic problems. Real needs and those of future generations can be provided for with an awakening of consciousness.

Hopefully, today under President Obama's administration, despite the problems of his first year in office, there is the possibility that not only will individuals acting together gain a measure of control over the political process, but each member of society will gain control of his or her own self-development for true happiness and well-being. Our democracy must protect each person both as an individual and as a social being.

Chapter Two
Mass Culture and Democracy

I

"Modern American consumer culture arose after 1890, the outcome of a synergy of economic and cultural forces."[1] Production and consumption were qualitatively different from the era before. The Industrial Revolution, by the end of the nineteenth century, was producing goods on a massive scale. "From convenience foods to clothing, appliances to automobiles, the enormous output of industrial production led businesses to coordinate methods of distribution and sales and to forge the infrastructure of our consumer culture."[2] There was an array of mail-order houses, chain stores syndicates, and department stores all in the name of commercialism.

It was the birth of advertising. A new professional and managerial class of college-educated, white-collar men came into existence with the purpose of creating advertising and marketing methods to increase sales and thus production by corporations. A new middle class formed in the interest of improving efficiency and controlling the economy. Mass consumption was promoted to increase production and the wealth of those in charge.

Women consumers became a class of their own, considering that much of the purchasing of goods and services for the household and family was done by the woman of the house. "Born at the same time, the 'organization man' and 'Mrs. Consumer' in many ways reprised the older dichotomy of manly producers and domestic women."[3] Women bought not only for the household, but also became avid readers of melodramas and novels for pleasure. Mass-circulation magazines, such as *Ladies Home Journal* and *Good Housekeeping*, were founded to foster a female culture of consumption. Leisure time was made available for housewives as well as for workers, who were rewarded with it for their production.

Yet, it was not until the 1950s that mass-consumption culture reached a peak due to United States prosperity. By that time, Americans lived in a leisure-time society. Mass culture reached a zenith for both men and women, despite the fact that women were not the equals of men in the United States socio-economic structure. Mass consumption managed a false equality through the satisfaction of created desires.

The public was convinced that the economy was operating in its best interest. As a result, the individual, male and female, willingly accepted the status quo of public policy and societal order. Individuals also supported the government without dissent, for the most part, so that corporations freely ran the economy to continue to provide more of the "good life," defined not by the individual but by advertising.

John Kenneth Galbraith wrote that the United States economy was, to a large extent, not a market system but a planned system. For corporations to produce standardized mass-consumption goods on a large scale, they had to organize, hire specialists to devise market strategies, and pursue government and public relations policies for the primary objective of self-growth. They had to control the market rather than be controlled by it, foreshadowing present-day affairs.

The market system, contrary to traditional belief, does not determine "winners" and "losers." According to Galbraith:

> "With the rise of the great corporation goes the power extensively to enforce its will on the society – not only to fix prices and costs but to influence consumers, and organize the supply of materials and components, a strategy for handling labor and influencing the attitudes of the community and the actions of the state...the purposes of its controlling intelligence, of its technostructure, became of the highest importance."[4]

For this reason, management power rose in relation to ownership. It had the finances, the skill, and the know-how to plan for growth, often at the expense of the "little man" in the domestic and international markets. This power to control contributed to its general ability to manipulate society. The public failed to realize it was being manipulated for private gain because it was pacified by advertising and media manipulation into a materialistic mentality placating them with consumption. People were taught by advertising and the media to want manufactured goods, which they paid for by mass producing them.

Dominant values of society were organized through consumption practices. "Thus, ...society (was and still is) described as materialistic, as more concerned with 'having' to the exclusion of 'being,' as commodified, as hedonistic, or more positively, as a society of choice and consumer sovereignty."[5]

A consumer society functions with little government regulation controlling American corporations and suppressing the market. In the United States, government policy gives the superstructure of production and sales the freedom needed to promote consumer spending. Consumer culture is frequently connected with mass consumption and is part of the inclusive term of mass culture. Freedom bears with it the disguise that everyone must be a consumer. There is no constraint on what can be consumed. Even the poor have ambitions and desires to obtain the goods and develop the social relations prevalent in affluent society. They want the "good life," the "American Dream." Desires are manipulated and irrationally promoted by advertising and the media.

In the United States, commercialism, as a false art form, reduces the reality of human needs by indoctrinating the public to irrationally produce goods that perpetuate social existence as is. People, including the underclasses, are led to seek what they "should want." Mass media advertising informs the consumer that he or she cannot live without the luxury items, which become part of the culture and deplete desperately needed resources.

Thus, the consumer desires and purchases not only basic necessities but fabricated desires as well, at times at the expense of real needs such as state of the art health care facilities. "Happiness" in the form of pleasure is defined for the individual in search of success. It is always beyond reach because the individual is programmed to always want more than he or she has or more than he or she is capable of becoming.

Because the superstructure of production informs workers what to produce, workers, instead of giving of themselves in creative production, follow orders as objects in the production process rather than as subjects in control of creative production. A blue collar worker no longer thinks about what he or she is producing, nor does a white collar employee care about the contents of a letter he or she is signing, but rather they are programmed to meet a quota. This helps society maintain an artificial guise that makes the whole social order seem rational when, in fact, it is irrationally based on a concept of meaningless individual submission to the production-consumption process.

The worker's reward for his production in a mass-consumption society is leisure time. Because goods can be produced at great speed and with little mental or physical effort, time is left over after the production process is completed, for the worker's idle indulgence of his or her desires. A lack of creativity results in failure of cultural development and positive innovation during leisure time. This is true not only of the worker, but also of the housewife in mass-consumption culture, who has many labor-saving devices at her disposal thus giving her "free" time to buy more.

Sociologist David Riesman, in the 1950s, stated in his essay, "Some Issues in the Future of Leisure," that the individual does not know what to do with this leisure and does not rationally plan how to best use it. Instead, as leisure time increases, he or she merely develops an increased desire to purchase more goods – not only different ones but also more of the same of what he or she already has.

Reisman points out in his essay, "Abundance for What," that the individual in mass-consumption society has few goals outside of consumption. The consumer does not act out of free will or independent decision-making. Instead, advertising convinces "mass man" to desire consumption. It does not matter what the individual consumes as long as he or she participates in the acquisition activity.

Advertising then, as well as today, reduces the reality of human needs through indoctrinating the public to irrationally produce and consume products that perpetuate the socio-economic system as it is. People are led to seek what they "should want" according to the superstructure society has created.

There is the problem of "keeping up with the Joneses." "Mass man" and woman want to keep up with others and surpass them. For example, the individual sees that his or her neighbor has a built-in swimming pool; his or her goal is not only to have one but to have a more elaborate and expensive one. "Mass man" goes on vacation not to be happy but to have fun. There is no enjoyment in viewing the scenery because the individual is all engrossed in taking pictures with a costly camera to "show off" to those he or she is trying to impress by capturing the scenery on film.

Mass media advertising informs consumers that they cannot live without the luxury items, which have become part of the culture, despite the depletion of vitally needed resources. Thus the individual consumes not only basic real needs but fabricated or false needs as well, often at the expense of the real needs. The consumer sees no difference between the two. As a result, resources were and are not now adequately conserved for the real needs of present and future generations. This includes not only natural resources but "man" as a human resource.

Our environmental crisis has steadily worsened without much public stress to force adequate environmental reforms on the part of government or industry. In general, American consumers living in today's society do not notice, or care a lot, if natural resources are depleted or misallocated until they are jarred out of their complacency in crisis times, such as gas shortages and price hikes. Market prices have risen, in general, and today put the country into a deep recession that government reforms will take a while to overturn even if they are instituted.

In American society today, the individual spends increasingly more time alone and far less time with friends in meaningful activity. "Mass man" does not go to the theater for an uplifting and soul-searching experience but seeks entertainment as a diversion.

The individual spends more time on the Internet or watching television and substitutes these activities for meaningful relationships with friends. While the individual avoids conflict from within his self-being or her self-being and criticism from the outside world, he or she also avoids personal development, meaningful commitments, and a search for the truth underlying many of life's fundamental questions.

Erich Fromm, in his book *The Sane Society*, describes the individual as essentially alone. He or she can attain a sense of identity only by truly sensing within him- or herself that "I am I."[6] This can only be accomplished by developing active powers to such an extent "that he can be related to the world without having to submerge in it; if he can achieve a productive orientation. The alienated person, however, tries to solve the problem in a different way; namely, by conforming. He feels secure in being as similar as possible to his fellow man…"[7]

The identity problems of "post-modern man" continue as long as free will is subordinated to the directives of a mass-consumption society. Furthermore, because it is possible to carry out banking, shopping, and work at home as a result of cable and satellite television and now through the Internet, "post-modern man" is more isolated than ever. Facebook does not change this.

In general, feelings are not part of an active consciousness in mass culture. They are the products of a passive mind that absorbs directives from the outside world. In essence, the individual proves he or she is a good American by participating in consumption for self-gratification.

As "mass man," the individual develops no self-standards nor does he or she question actions or motives. Instead, people become unhappy with feelings of guilt if they do not measure up to the mainstream of society. Ideology became propaganda and religion, dogma. Television programs of meaningful content or of a controversial nature are not aired because advertisers fail to sponsor them. The end result of all of this is conformism and crowd behavior.

According to the findings of David Riesman, applicable to today, the content of media reduces all meaning to the objective of achieving self-gratification. The search for ideals is replaced by a process that rationalizes pleasure. People want to personalize their relationships with the performers and politicians because meaningful relationships do not exist for them in society. Since the audience emphasizes the quality of sincerity, it does not have to deal with the content of the performance or the issues of a political campaign. It can remain passive. Thus, irrational or false relationships are established that take the place of meaningful relationships on a personal level.

Apathetic conformism and emotional crowd behavior, both evident in American society today, are not conducive to the rational, pragmatic application of democratic principles in finding solutions to economic, political, and social problems. United States democracy is jeopardized to the extent that "mass man" lives a passive and alienated existence. In this state, the individual is incapable of the critical thinking needed to preserve democracy and keep it viable in light of the crises facing it.

The individual cannot judge reality if language – including that of the ideological principles underlying democracy – is neutralized for the purpose of control. The individual cannot determine the gap between democracy as theory and democracy as practiced today if he or she does not know there is a contradiction. All is reduced to bland acceptance.

The individual must know that expert opinions in government are not always valid unless they are based upon substantial factual information and sound judgmental experience. The individual cannot rationally judge information as long as the media of mass communication do not serve in a critical capacity to reveal the truth – as long as they merely report what they are told without questioning their sources.

"Mass man" has been noted by David Reisman as "other-directed" in contrast to the "inner-directed" man or woman of earlier periods. The behavior of the inner-directed person was governed by internal norms or values. His or her activity in life was directed by the values – largely imposed by parents, school, and church – that came to form the content of his or her conscience. The "other-directed" man or woman, on the other hand, does not internalize values but rather seeks approval of others and becomes part of a meaningless crowd that follows the directions of the consumer market.

In the politics of mass democracy, these qualities affect the relationship between the politician and the electorate. As part of the crowd, the consumer as citizen accepts generalized phrases spewed out by politicians as truth emphasizing that things are good, and that there is no reason to worry.

The tremendous influence mass media has on voter opinion results in irrational responsiveness, if any. Political policy platforms are presented to the public by the media in a compromised and overly simplified form that placates the vested interests needed for a candidate to win an election. Winning – not the issues – is most often the reason for entering an election.

In mass democracy the language of public relations advertising manipulates the public to vote a certain way on an issue without ever knowing what the issue really is or what the ramifications of policy enactment are. Because of this, the voter elects a politician into office more often on the basis of personal appeal and apparent sincerity rather than on his or her policy stand. Democracy is a term when referred to at all by the media or politicians is used as rhetoric to win voter approval. It serves to inspire and win support without having any rational connection to ethical values.

The United States political process itself does not constitute an infringement of democracy. Its misuse does. To a certain extent, political compromise is necessary to ensure that the political process remains stable in spite of the conflicts associated with a pluralistic society. Also, informal and formal interest groups can provide the powerless with the influence they need to be heard politically.

Yet in mass culture, compromise often prevents issues from having any ethical value. Meaning is often compromised out of existence. Rational and ethical decision-making does not take place out of fear of losing the election game. Also, groups can become crowds acting irrationally and irresponsibly with no ethical or reasonable goal in mind. The public decides whom to vote for on the basis of personality and looks, rather than on the basis of real issues. Often, voter decisions are based on who gets more of the economic pie.

Those in control of the nation's wealth and resources have a stake in downplaying democratic ethics, which could induce a moral awakening to alter the status quo. Corporate conglomerates exercise enormous economic power under government sanction; therefore, when democratic principles are referred to by some elected officials or those seeking office, they are often in the form of propaganda used to gain public approval and compliance to the status quo power structure of government and corporate America.

For example, President George W. Bush catered to the corporate world, in particular to oil interests, with his economic "trickle down" theory of helping corporations expand by tax relief. This supposedly would improve the lot of the working class through free enterprise and increased production. Instead of improving the lot of most Americans, he brought the country "down" to an enormous recession. The wealthy got richer, and the middle class and working class got poorer.

The politician in mass society assumes the role of representing the interests of his or her constituents rather than dealing with the issues affecting the broader community or the nation as a whole. In the legislature, the politician makes deals to trade off or bargain with in order to fulfill constituents' desires. When constituents' interests are in conflict the representative acts as a neutral middleman seeking to work out compromise arrangements satisfactory to all. Public relation firms are hired to create the public face of the politician to appease neglected constituent issues.

Campaigns may be based on promises to do good for everybody, or they may appeal to bigotry and fear. Slogans, such as "A Square Deal" or "Get the Country Moving Again," abound. All this is aimed at getting out the vote. They attempt to capture a mood among the electorate that will generate the greatest favorable appeal without alienating many voters.

Issues are not rationally presented but rather are camouflaged to make them appear the way the politician and the public relations representatives want them presented. The idea is to win the crowd's approval, often to compromise issues out of existence. Through political advertising the public is coaxed into buying a candidate into office. The aim is to maintain the status quo rather than to introduce reform.

Under the Administration of President Ronald Reagan, mass culture reached a new zenith. This has carried on over the years despite the fact that the economy reached a new low during the George W. Bush Administration, in which the country was driven into a virtual recession. Also, during the Bush years, the environment was depleted as a result of the power of the super-rich oil conglomerates. It must be noted that even during the Administrations of President Jimmy Carter and President Bill Clinton, mass culture prevailed, even though tax cuts were not the thing of the day, and free spending was not given a nod from the government.

Hopefully, President Barack Obama, with executive orders based on new ethics rules that result in such policies as shutting down detention camps that practice torture, can lead United States democracy in a rational and ethical direction. Only time will tell if we have entered a true creedal passion period.

II

Creedal passion did occur in the 1960s and 1970s, despite the elements in control of mass society's status quo. Tensions existed over issues of race and gender. In 1972 Congress sent the Equal Rights Amendment to the states for ratification, and in 1973 the Supreme Court invalidated most state laws criminalizing a woman's access to abortion in the historic Roe v. Wade decision. The hippy culture, free love, prevalent use of drugs, and disenchantment with the Vietnam War resulted in peaceful and violent demonstrations and racial riots, all in opposition to the military industrial complex controlling the political and governmental scenes. Yet, this was but an aberration in American history. Society moved back to maintaining the status quo.

In mass culture, dark images of treason and excess of the 1960s were not difficult to find. "There was the fable of the doubly-victimized soldiers in Vietnam, betrayed first by liberals and doves in government and then spat upon by members of the indistinguishable New Left/Counterculture."[9] It resulted in outrage. The conservatives won their point.

James T. Patterson writes in his book *Restless Giant* that mainstream culture was the standard account of the decade. Mainstream culture was tepid, mechanical, and uniform; while the revolt of youth against it was a joyous and even a great cultural flowering, until it quickly became mainstream.

Most Americans were not as interested in politics as they were in the consumer goods they felt they had to have to maintain an adequate lifestyle.

By the mid-1970s there were:

"Microwave ovens, fully programmable pocket calculators, and automatic icemakers in refrigerators. The first bar codes greeted shoppers in stores. Automatic teller machines, introduced a few years earlier, were slowly increasing in numbers and rendering obsolete the constraints of 'bankers' hours. Touch-tone phones, an innovation of the 1960s, were spreading rapidly and replacing dials."[10]

Also, consumers had a wide range of automobiles from which to choose. There was a virtual explosion of cars on the roads.

Suburban mall developers asserted control and homogeneity as is typical of mass culture. The stores met the needs of mass society, and storeowners maximized profits. Suburban growth has defined modern America since

1970 when, for the first time in our history, more people lived in the suburbs than in the cities. Surrounding the urban areas were roads congested by traffic jams; superhighways proliferated the United States terrain. All of this occurred as consumerism flourished, despite the fact that the American economy was declining, exposing the limits of the New Deal and the Great Society welfare states. Mass-consumption culture was firmly entrenched with no effective opposition present.

The more people bought the more they wanted and the more they wanted the more wants became fabricated needs. The public, in general, wanted what the rich and famous had. This was true of the poor and underclass income strata members as well as of the middle class. They marveled at what was out of reach and dreamt of having the lucrative "American Dream" for themselves someday.

As the 1970s passed into the Reagan Administration of the 1980s, the economy brightened. More and better consumer goods appeared on the market. Families lived in bigger houses. VCRs and personal computers were dominating the scene. "By the early 1990s, Americans owned nearly a billion credit cards, which they used with an abandon that ratcheted up personal debt."[11] Yet, the more people could afford, they more they wanted and the more dissatisfied they became.

There was no attempt at inner-selfhood development. There was no sense of personal satisfaction. There was no interest in the effect this was having on democracy's intrinsic values. There was no real interest in politics. Reagan basked in the glow of the material world he helped create with tax cuts and runaway inflation. He attributed his success to his fiscal policies and deregulatory moves that spurred market activity and investment.

A goal of the Reagan Era was to get rid of excessive regulation. The result of deregulation and reduced oversight was epitomized by Wall Street's Michael Robert Milken of Drexel Bernham Lambert. He developed high yield bonds, also called junk bonds. He received over one billion dollars by 1990. In 1989 he was indicted by a federal grand jury for racketeering and fraud and pled guilty. He was sentenced to ten years in prison, paid a total of $ 900,000,000 in fines and settlements and was released from prison, still a billionaire, after 22 months in jail at the end of George Bush's presidency in January 1993.

According to Patterson, the Reagan years ended up advancing two trends that covered the following three decades. First, people became convinced that politics was "nasty." Partisan politics had become vicious in the rhetoric it spewed out to the public. "Encouraged by a more strident media culture, many candidates and officeholders plunged into a political culture of clamorous sound-bite communications and became increasingly uncompromising..."[12] The second trend was that the government became divided, pitting a Congress of Democrats against a Republican presidency.

It was the age of media politics that became more and more pronounced as time moved on. Managers and pollsters presented candidates in the images that would win votes. Large sums of money were spent to win elections. Politics became a process of mass consumerism with candidates being the products promoted to sell. Grassroots efforts to get out the vote in an attempt to represent the people declined.

Critics of Reagan attacked him as promoting materialism and the greedy upwardly mobile professional class of "yuppies." Becoming "successful" by playing the corporate game of "climbing the ladder" toward bigger promotions led to the purchase of more expensive houses and cars as well as all the other trappings of wealth. Unfortunately, this did not bring contentment. It led to more and more "backstabbing" and disregard of ethical standards. "Mass man" became less – not more – content. By the 1990s, more and more wants had become false needs.

Unfortunately, tax cuts during the Reagan years were not well thought out but led instead to ballooning deficits. It was the Clinton tax increases that led to the strong economy of the 1990s. Yet, "mad" consumerism did not decline. Many Americans remained "hyper-competitive and materialistic people who often compensated for feelings of spiritual emptiness by lusting after possessions, drinking excessively, and engaging in promiscuous sex."[13]

The United States has become a utopia of consumer goods such as VCRs and DVDs, color television, air-conditioning, personal computers and Internet access. Consumer choice expanded to the point that the shoppers reported being anxious over catalog choices of products. More and more Americans reached the upper-middle and upper classes. Yet, people were restless. They continued to want more and more of what was beyond their reach to afford. Advertising reached a peak as it attempted to capitalize on the trend that had begun decades ago to program "mass man" to want false needs or created desires.

With the George W. Bush Administration, tax cuts were again instituted to the benefit of the super rich. Bush and his supporters deceived the public into believing that this would eventually lead to increased investments by those receiving the cuts, so that the workforce would gradually benefit. It did not.

The conservative Congress became enfeebled and corrupt. The country was pushed into what became a recession. President Bush and his Administration had to cover up the fact that they primarily supported the rich. Tax cuts were billed as a way to return "surplus" taxes to the economy. When the surplus disappeared, they were remarketed as a stimulus measure.

The press, wary of seeming partisan, reported the claims of both parties rather than analyzing them. Unfortunately, the liberals were too weak in producing a new economic policy to counteract the Bush disaster. Conservatives pursued an economic policy that expanded the wealth of the very rich without any effective opposition by liberal Democrats or the press.

Mass-consumption culture did not die. Consumers wished to emulate the very rich. Corruption prevailed with scandals in politics and corporate America. The whole world has moved more steadily away from liberal economic policies toward less regulation and freer markets.

Consumer spending is finally decreasing because much of the public can barely afford necessities such as gas and food. It is a fact that today the rich got richer and leaving 99.99% of the population behind with a flat income.

With the bottom dropping out of the stock market, even the super rich are suffering today and investor corruption is slowly being uncovered. It is yet to be seen what the Obama Administration can do to rectify conditions.

Individuals still want to be part of the crowd. Shopping on the Internet e-Bay (the world's largest on-line marketplace) remains relatively high, as more and more people spend time alone on their computers. Unfortunately, this is causing alienation, anomie, boredom, and depression for much of the American and international public, complicating their lives and livelihoods.

Chapter Three
The Mass Media

I

Despite the fact that the individual appears to be happy in mass culture, in many cases he or she is, in fact, alienated from his or her inner selfhood. The individual no longer has the ability to originate an opinion of external reality as a subject self. The mass person cannot negate as false what he or she sees nor exhibit a will for change. Consciousness is determined from outside the individual's being largely by the mass media.

Mental and emotional problems result because the individual's thought process is suppressed. A subjective awareness is necessary for the inner selfhood of the individual to negate the external reality of mass culture. There is a need for the liberation of consciousness in the individual.

Art can serve a critical function in society for the individual to criticize mass culture and find inner peace and positive direction. It can teach the individual to look beyond the given and reach for potential differences or change. It can teach people to sublimate to awe-inspiring heights.

Unfortunately, in mass culture, commercialism is the generally accepted art form. Art is reduced to a "sales pitch" that promotes increased consumption on the basis that "happiness" will be bought if the individual participates in the market system. In fact, inner happiness or well-being is replaced by superficial pleasure or "having fun."

Thus, in mass culture art achieves an irrational use value promoting passivity in society and perpetuating the institutional order or "way of doing things." In mass culture, the critical nature of art is lost. The accepted art world becomes a process of desublimating the negative or critical.

Avant-garde art is a struggle against this one-dimensional (as Herbert Marcuse calls it in his book *One-Dimensional Man*) cultural assimilation of art into society. It is tolerated to the extent that it is also largely ignored and thus poses no threat in its critical separateness from mass society. The dialectical antagonism to commercialism is practiced only to a minor extent.

One of the reasons that this pacification has taken place is the very size of society, not only in terms of the viewer audience but also in terms of the very large-scale management and distribution of the media. All pressures and disagreements are assimilated within the organizational structure so that the end product has reduced all antagonisms to a one-dimensional passivity.

As a result, the content of media reduces all meaning to the objective of achieving self-gratification. The search for ideals is replaced by a process of rationalizing pleasure. Even the true value of a meaningful love relationship is reduced to the fulfillment of sexual satisfaction.

The mass media of communications promote an attitude of tolerance based upon the pacification of language and, subsequently, thought. This function permeates into the "selling" of political candidates for office. There is a tendency to identify prevailing beliefs as absolute definitions of democracy. Furthermore, politicians tend to promise to "do good" for everybody for the sole purpose of winning elections. The face of a politician is an image constructed by the public-relations firm hired to win.

The value criteria in judging entertainment is no longer based upon intrinsic worth but upon the sales pitch of the performer. Content of performance is not important. Rather, the appearance of sincerity by the performer determines his or her worth. Such is true of a political campaign in which personality rather than issues, never controversial, determines the winner. The media sell candidates for office as if they were consumer goods. They promote an attitude of tolerance and an absence of the negative by using language that pacifies the audience.

People want to personalize their personal relationships with performers and politicians because meaningful relationships do not exist for them in society. In general, people do not see each other as subject individuals to have a lasting relationship with but as objects to serve a purpose such as pleasure or use.

Since the audience emphasizes the appearance of sincerity, it does not have to deal with the content of the performance or the issues of a political campaign. It can remain passive, enjoying a false relationship with a candidate. An irrational relationship is established that takes the place of having meaningful relationships in society on a personal level.

The function of the media editor is to placate advertisers, newspaper guild contractors, and distributors, as well as to satisfy the audience. The chief strategy of the media is to introduce and rationalize changes, improvements, or discontinuities in tastes and conventions. The media have a stake in promoting desires. They cannot afford to have the masses too attached to a particular taste because they may have to alter it for greater profit if sales decline or don't meet expectations.

The use value of the mass media "art form" is in its ability to sustain a faith in the irrationality of mass production and mass consumption culture. Commercialism must create a public that thinks it is happy to suit irrational behavior on a moment-to-moment basis. Pleasure is momentary; happiness is not.

The media do not educate; they placate. David Riesman states in "The Oral Tradition, the Written Word, and the Screen Image" that while the mass media are replacing written literature on an ever-increasing scale, the degree to which they serve the same educational function as literature is much less.

The mass media of television and radio aim at appeal rather than at education. It is obvious that the alienation and pacification of modern man would be much less severe if literature as art form were allowed to regain control of social development by presenting sublimated ideals to aim for and lasting relationships to emulate, as it had decades ago. The media and, of course, now the Internet have taken over the socialization function of maintaining passivity.

For example, many students use the media brilliantly in writing. Yet, they lack the ability to create clear and extended narratives, according to Professor Donald Roberts of Stanford University. Their writing does not necessarily present forceful arguments. The media aim at "the masses"; they do not produce individualization or critical thought.

Neither does the Internet, which aims at equalizing users of the Web into being a sort of sameness. Entertainers become friends. This promotes passiveness on the part of the viewers or listeners. On the other hand, literature does not allow characters to become friends unless a reader critically understands the characters.

II

In the United States the media and the politicians have been in a symbiotic relationship since the 1950s. "Presidential politics has evolved in quadrennial leaps and bounds since television first made its presence felt in the battles for the White House in 1952, bringing the Democratic and Republican national conventions into America's living rooms a scant six months after the coaxial cable had been laid from coast to coast."[1]

During the 1980s, President Ronald Reagan used television to portray himself in a favorable light – and he did it brilliantly. The goal of television coverage was to present the President's greatest asset, which his aides called "his personality." It incorporated his disarming actor's smile. He was presented with a confident air and a Marlboro Man walk, a leader deserving a following. The media erased his negatives.

Reagan countered the memory of unpopular issues by choosing activities that even contradicted his policies. For example, he presented himself at the handicapped Olympics and at the opening ceremony of an old-age home with no hint whatsoever of the fact that he tried to cut budgets for the disabled and for federally subsidized housing for the elderly.

"President Reagan (was) accused of running a campaign in which he highlight(ed) the images and (hid) from the issues. But there (was) no evidence that the charge hurt him because when people (saw) the President on television he (made) them feel good, about America, about themselves, and about him."[2] All in all, the media manipulated facts to suit the purpose of presenting Reagan in a favorable light. This is true of the media and politics in general today.

The public was, and still is, presented with managed manipulation of facts by politicians and media experts. This is not conducive to presenting reality needed by citizens to vote effectively and to have a representative democratic government.

Yet there is hope. Cable News Network has at times appealed to a reasoning audience. CNN in their weekly analysis and interview shows provides important forums for politicians and policies to be examined in depth. Also, the Public Broadcasting System provides the public with insight into public policies and the officials who make and carry them out. For example, "The MacNeil/Lehrer Newshour (gave) America sufficient breadth, great depth, and a refreshingly nonhuckstering approach to the nightly news. Other shows such as Frontline are often masterful and deserving of the accolades that come their way."[3]

While the network-television news broadcasters have a far-reaching reputation, it is the local shows that carry the biggest influence in our major media markets. Local television shows are closer to the heart of the audience in mass culture. They appeal more easily to emotions because they touch on local human interest stories instead of informing the public of crucial hardcore news information in the United States and globally that would be difficult for an audience to relate to without using reasoning. News is mixed with items that make viewers "happy."

"Not only do local stations have more viewers, they also have many more hours of news each week. Local stations have anywhere from three to four hours of news a day—and some do even more. There is at least a half hour in the morning, at least a half hour at noon, and at least a half hour at night. Networks, of course, have a half-hour of prime-time news in the evenings and have their morning shows, portions of which are given to news but most to entertainment and so on in the waking hours of most of America."[4]

Thus, local news appeals to emotions by replacing the rational presentation of important facts on the national and international level. Instead of paying attention to long and even short-term issues of prime importance to his or her being, the mass viewer buys what is thrilling and titillating on the television screen. The media sell what viewers are willing to buy when they tune in to their channels of interest.

It is a fact of mass culture in most cases that the messenger – the anchorman or woman – is more important to the average audience than the facts of a news item. The more difficult it is to determine the quality of a news story, the more important the messenger becomes. "The more interpretation is involved, the more likely it will be that a print story will have a byline, and the more likely that a TV news story will be presented by a well-known reporter or anchor."[5] This simplifies reality by appealing to emotions rather than reason.

The presence of the reporter, for example, every night on a television channel's news hour, encourages habitual viewing. This is true of bylines given in a daily news column. The bias presented by the messenger appeals to a certain audience and draws in the money needed for funding. As is true of mass society in general, the appeal of a bias is an appeal to the emotions rather than to reason. Furthermore, the financial gain for the network may come at the expense of better alternatives such as funding additional informative news programming.

With the advent of the Internet, which is even cheaper than cable, "bloggers can be narrowly focused and even more partisan than cable channel pundits. The smaller the break-even audience and the lower the cost, the more distinct the viewpoint—and hence the more vehement the charges of bias"[6] made by those using reason to criticize the practice.

The more competition among news providers to appeal to an audience, the less often viewers will be presented with the hard-core news programming they should have to live effectively in the world. Instead, they are presented with human interest stories they can relate to.

Networks follow the pack to draw in the advertising money an audience brings with it. They pour money into the personalities and stories that appeal to a target audience. As more channels arise, and more anchors present the same stories, news budgets are spread so thin in the competition that important and expensive stories and investigative reporting are often unaffordable.

"Soft news" is increasingly replacing "hard news" to elevate the selling capacity of news making news appeal to the emotions of the audience. Soft news emphasizes the human impact it will have on "mass man." When the news does report on foreign affairs, it does so by making an appeal to a new audience that replaces one that listens to hard news.

"When soft news covers a war, it focuses more on the human drama than on the geopolitical stakes, foreign relations, and diplomacy. A rescued hostage, a downed pilot, bereaved families, or a national guardsman resentful of the better-armed regular forces will get extensive coverage; congressional hearings, budget fights, and meetings with allies may go unmentioned."[7]

"Advertisers particularly value viewers aged 18-49, especially women."[8] That is because they make new consumer decisions and spend money. Mass culture wins. The news sells by appealing to issues the consumer is willing to buy. It deals with right and wrong, good and evil. For example, President George W. Bush created an emotional frenzy by referring to Saddam Hussein as "evil" in order to gain public support for the Iraq War.

Most people in today's society believe they know the difference between right and wrong and deal with issues in those terms without reasoning on the basis of hard facts before drawing conclusions.

"Soft news doesn't bring people to politics by enlightening them; it does so by connecting their world to the human interest and drama in politics. Soft news ignores primaries and off-year elections and covers more crime and education and war than was the norm on hard news shows. Nor does it cover all scandals; a personal scandal like the Monica Lewinsky affair was ideal for it, whereas Whitewater, a complex sets of financial deals was barely mentioned."[9]

What is happening in mass culture is that the inconsequential but appealing issues have replaced a factual presentation of important news issues. The audience attaches itself to the anchorman or woman rather than rationally trying to extract from a news item the depth of its meaning. While local human interest stories may bring more people to the TV or cable program, they fail to focus on main events of importance to the nation and the rest of the world. News has become a commodity that "mass man" buys by listening to, relating to, and conforming to even if it is negative news. Soft news distracts from relevant, often crucial, facts by satisfying the consumer audiences' taste for its the purpose of increasing coverage and increasing revenue.

Chapter Four
The Internet

I

Contemporary society has entered the postmodern era. The Internet has brought with it a new age. It serves as a fantastic means for obtaining information and making contacts. Yet for many of its users, it poses psychological problems, sometimes serious.

"The Postmodern economy can be characterized as far more consumption-oriented, relying on media and sophisticated marketing techniques to offer not simply products, but 'lifestyles' or social identities dependent on these products and appealing to consumer desire and fear. To provide the illusion of consumer choice among similar luxury items, the advertising and public relations apparatus attempts to create and sustain arbitrary hierarchies of taste and fashion."[1] Through its language it attempts to present one product brand as superior to another while in fact there is little, if any, difference.

Because the postmodern individual lives in a mobile society, there are ads in shopping malls, auto centers, on TV and the computer to attract him or her to consume the advertised product or service. We are suffering from ad creep and ad clutter. In the 1970s the consumer listened to or read about 500 ads a day. This is in contrast to 5000 now. They appear on buses, buildings, public floors as well as in the ordinary media and on the Internet. This is an assault on the senses. As a result, many consumers have developed a negative reaction to them and are alienated from them. Thus, advertisers have had to decide how to supersaturate consumers with these ads; for example, placing them in subway tunnels to regain attention.

The ads must be more creative to compete with others. They have the power to sell as long as they don't turn people off. Advertisers aim at entertaining without a full frontal assault, and they aim at presenting ads as novelties; for example, buying ad space to appear in urinals. Brand names appear in the form of large logos, for example, on clothing. There is direct demographic and psychological marketing via the mail, telephone and the Internet. The Internet is an important source that ad people have tapped. Computers even appear in hotel lobbies, hotel rooms, and beauty salons. Many advertising techniques now blur previous demarcations between ad and news or entertainment for the purpose of making sales.

"As such, these factors combine to negate old barriers between private sphere of individual and family life, and the public's sphere of the marketplace, banking facilities and investment houses. The advent of the home office or even computer access to the Internet clouds the distinctions between work and leisure."[2] Consumers welcome this and avidly purchase new cell phones, televisions and computer hookups.

As a result of aggressive new marketing techniques and strategies, there is an economic shift to a new "market society." The pursuit of private gain becomes an all-encompassing activity of social life. "In market society all other principles of social organization become subordinated to the overreaching one of private gain."[3] Greed overtakes human endeavors. In other words, the market is overtaking the selfhood of the rational and ethical individual through the promotion of irrational mass consumption as reality.

With the phenomenon of the Internet, culture has taken a turn, becoming not only for the masses but also by the masses, as Lee Siegel points out in his book, *Against the Machine*. Leisure time is no longer for buying and selling. Rather, it is the process of buying and selling.

In Alvin Toffler's *Third Wave*, all of the individual's existence is spent turning into a commodity or service that someone else will want to acquire.[4] The individual becomes a more extensive "mass man." He or she not only is the object of ads, but produces goods at the same time. Mass consumption and mass production are concurrent.

For example, to cut the costs of purchasing a table, the individual purchases parts over the Internet and assembles it. Leisure time is spent in the process of labor. Thus, the individual produces at the same time as consuming. Using Toffler's terminology this is a "prosumption process." There is no real leisure time for those engaged in this activity. Mass production replaces leisure time in the individual's activity of mass consumption.

Leisure time is saturated with economic urgency. "Once we recognize that much of our so-called leisure time is, in fact, spent producing goods and services for our own use – presuming – then the old distinction between work and leisure falls apart."[5] For example, the process of bidding for commodities on eBay turns leisure into work and free time into a commercial process.

The individual is in a sense subservient to the marketplace rather than in charge of creatively producing goods as a subject. His or her identity is merged with the production-consumption process. People are alienated from themselves to a deeper extent than those participating in standard production-consumption.

"Internet culture is all about finding a clique or group and striving to reproduce its style with your own adorable, unthreatening, superficial twist."[6] The individual is drawn to what everyone else likes in an attempt to satisfy the needs and tastes of others. He or she strives for popularity as part of the masses rather than for fame through uniqueness, genius, or talent. The reason for "bigness" or popularity doesn't matter.

The individual is alienated from him- or herself in the process of striving to be the "other" as much as possible in mass culture. "Mass man" is separated as an object from his or her subject development or selfhood. The crowd is all that matters at the expense of individual initiative.

Consumer culture is enhanced through the use of credit cards or plastic money. Vast amounts of wealth are rapidly accumulated and lost, not by oil wells or factories, but through speculative activities such as acquisitions and mergers or "derivative fiscal instruments as exemplified by currencies, secondary contracts, options and corporate bonds, traded globally and twenty-four hours per day…Practices such as online 'day trading' by unlicensed speculators has added to the volatility and casino-like atmosphere of such markets."[7] Some Internet stocks, such as Amazon.com, have exploded in so-called value without ever realizing any true value. This information economy has become volatile, leading to consumer anxiety by distant events in far away places in which commodities are manufactured.

One of the great paradoxes of the new economy is that stock valuations rise as corporations downsize their full-time employees or hire cheaper labor from far away – even authoritarian countries such as police-state regimes in Asia and South America. The work ethic is disintegrating as a result. There is no self-esteem generated from producing a "good" product. Loyalty by workers and corporations is disappearing. Value lies in producing cheaply to generate sales.

Furthermore, advertising such as in shopping malls has poorer Americans comparing themselves to more affluent owners and envying them. Alienation from society holds true of those who can't have but want what is advertised. Anomie increases with the lack of any sense of value. Ennui affects those who have and want more because they are bored. There is a loss of value and self-love on the part of those who all embrace consumerism.

The new economic age brings with it speed, efficiency and greater reach of communications with cable and satellite television, cell phone/beeper/pager systems, and the Internet. Yet, there are broad negative social implications at the expense of the new age of choice. Independence, flexibility, and connectivity give way to restricted audiences molded by the newer media delivering information, which may produce special-interest 'cyberspace' communities but at the expense of social cohesion of the larger society.

"The Internet, as postmodern medium par excellence, connects literally millions of people daily, but the communicative value of messages posted on web pages or chat rooms generally sustains little more than the fleeting impermanence of oral, conversational communication; individual web pages themselves scarcely survive for more than 90 days."[8] There is no permanence. This contributes to anxiety and alienation on the part of the average participant. The individual has entered a new era of evolutionary history in which rapid change is a dominant consequence.

With the advent of the Internet, problems of mass culture have not declined but, rather, have increased. While the Internet is phenomenal in providing information at the touch of the computer key and serves the purpose of making needed contacts in a split second, crowd behavior has been augmented with the disregard for leadership expertise and heroism. Each person is expressing his or her opinion equally with no concern for the individual's expertise or know-how. Each opinion is equal in worth but rarely in reality, so this is a misconception. The activity of the object "other" is the behavior the individual as object strives to emulate. He or she acts to be a part of the larger object whole. Hence, there is crowd behavior with no subject leader possessing the expertise to make the decisions other subjects can appreciate and follow.

Furthermore, the individual is alone more of the time as virtual relationships replace real ones. People actually work during their leisure time rather than use it for sublimating and creating works of art, which are instead replaced by egalitarian self-expression. Privacy is being invaded by the swiftness of the Internet, which leaves no time to reflect and cause self-development. The danger to democracy is that anyone in society can purchase a gun over the Internet and use it for any purpose including joining terrorist cells by simply tuning in to a jihad website.

Whether the Internet has a positive or negative social impact depends upon the quality of people's online activities and what the individual gives up to spend time online. The access to the Internet could increase people's social involvement as the telephone did. It could facilitate the formation of new relationships, social identity, and commitment among otherwise isolated individuals by distant or marginal members and political mobilization. It could aid in political involvement.

Yet, the ease of Internet communication encourages people to spend more time alone, or forming superficial relationships at the expense of face-to-face discussions and companionship with friends and family. The Internet is the first social environment to serve the needs of the isolated, elevated, asocial individual. "More and more people are able to live in a comfortable and complete self-enclosure than ever before."[9]

Increased numbers of people in the United States are interconnected by cell phones and e-mail than ever before. "Yet, 33% have fewer friends than twenty years ago. In general, the individual has only two friends today as opposed to three in 1985."[10] When asked in a recent television news survey, teenagers said that virtual friendships are just as good as real friends. This is not true. Real friends are individual beings who do not dissolve if the computer is turned off. They are part of our social environment and of our social interconnection and are necessary for democracy to flourish, protecting individual rights within the social setting.

Increasing numbers of people are dependent upon the Internet. Stock prices and sales of Google, MySpace, and Yahoo, for example, are rising at phenomenal rates. "There are currently about seventy million blogs in existence, with between forty thousand and fifty thousand being created every day."[11] These include political blogs, cultural blogs, and blogs for sex addicts. "Seventy million people are continuously engaged in presenting their general reflections and private thoughts in public, for other people."[12] This is all in an attempt on the part of individuals to be liked and to show themselves as the same as others but with their characteristics added to the mass. In this case people need others to prove their worth. There is no inner identity projected outward to other members of society. The individual is an object among other objects with no subject self-development, no responsibility, and no initiative. One is alienated from one's self itself.

"In fact, since the blogosphere represents mass opinion galvanized by the promise of approval and recognition, it is more a mainstream form of communication than the so-called mainstream media ever were."[13] In fact "big" media are attempting to go online to save their dwindling sales of newspapers and magazines, starve off bankruptcy, and possibly improve ad sales.

In the spring of 2007, the Federal Trade Commission moved to block Whole Foods half-billion dollar bid to buy out its leading competitor, Wild Oats because it found that John P. Mackey, the chief executive of Whole Foods Market, had disguised his identity to make a great number of postings on Yahoo's stock message boards before 2010. To chat-room regulars, this attempt to gain support for one's position is known as "sock puppetry." This is an example of how journalism has resulted in greed and pettiness as a result of efforts at anonymity and to avoid responsibility.

In some cases, the Internet drives people further into themselves, creating an inner emptiness by cutting the self off from reality. The individual seeks an escape from freedom in the anonymity of the crowd. By allowing individuals to appeal to the mass, the Internet is fostering a mass consciousness. Identity is lost in the anonymity of the crowd.

On the Internet, an impulse is only seconds away from its gratification. The individual does not get to have a feeling before sharing that feeling. According to psychologist Al Cooper, "the Internet provides immediate gratification that affects one's ability to inhibit previously managed drives and desires. In other words, the Internet creates the ideal consumer."[15] There is no time for subjective reflection or internal value decision-making. The individual is inundated with feelings as if consuming superimposed relationships.

The mass person seeks to escape the freedom of making choices by the anonymity of the crowd. In the conformity of mass society, the individual is making a social adjustment.

Individuals adjust to the expectations of the "other" – of the crowd. Ennui and anomie are engendered by living the alienated way of life, of losing selfhood to the anonymity of the crowd. Suicide can follow when "mass man" no longer considers life worth living.

"The psychic task, which a person can and must set for himself, is not to feel secure but to be able to tolerate insecurity, without panic and undue fear."[16] People must reaffirm their selfhoods whether using the Internet or not. Individuals must experience themselves as active beings with powers of their own, rather than being dependent on powers from outside. In an ethical and rational democracy uncertainty fosters self-questioning, which results in self-development. This is not true of mass culture in which the individual is living with anxiety over being unable to get more and more goods and services as well as being obsessed over achieving success within the status quo.

Another problem the Internet has confronted its users with is that art no longer serves as a sublimation process. The individual cannot project his or her consciousness away from the pressures of self-interest to project into an ideal awe-inspiring thing of beauty, as art should.

Instead, "mass man" becomes part of the work of creation. Commercial culture is all about the gratification of self-interest, and involves the total engagement of the ego. In other words, there is no projected reach by the subject into the sublime, into what could be, but a process of being an object among other objects, a process of being accepted by others to perpetuate what is comfortable.

Culture today needs authoritative institutions like a powerful newspaper, both to protect critical, independent spirits and to make sure that rational and ethical voices get heard in the louder din of more powerful economic and political entities promoting a mass life-style.

Bloggers often play into the hands of the powerful who want nothing to do with a critical and scrutinizing media. They seek to maintain themselves as is.

Independent thinking on the part of the subject individual to judge objective circumstances by understanding what experts are presenting as facts does not take place. The individual is an object among other objects acting out without informed sources offering alternatives to what is wrong or irrational. "Mass man" expresses his or her opinion as truth. Expertise is shunned. Being like the other is the supreme value. People are the same with each presenting him- or herself more like the other than the other. They strive for sameness.

To shun expertise means to shun the subject's individualism needed to manage different jobs in society, in some cases, important positions. Subject individuals are needed to interpret what politicians and officeholders are doing in order to defend democracy and to interpret whether or not the politicians' actions are really in the interest of democracy as an ideal applied to the real circumstances. Individual citizens attempting to be objects like other people in society is crowd behavior of no benefit to anyone. In many instances it can be harmful to others such as in the growth of terrorist cells where responsibility for one's own actions is shunned in the name of Islam.

Furthermore, as sociologist Ernest Becker points out:

> "The heroics of the visible world are as fragile as are all material things, as limited as a single life span; these are easily undermined with them. The crisis of middle- and upper-class youth in the social and economic structure of the Western world is precisely a crisis of belief in the vitality of the hero-systems that are offered by contemporary materialistic society. The young no longer feel heroic in doing as their elders did, and that's that."[17]

Alienation worsens because of scandals such as that of Enron, the huge energy giant, whose corporate officers took deductions in debt carried on its books as shareholder's equity in its stress on growth, or such as that of House Majority Leader Tom Delay violating campaign finance laws, and the sex scandal of Florida Congressman Mark Foley. Bernard Madoff, former Chairman of the Nasdeq Stock Market, was arrested and found guilty of running a "Ponzi scheme" securities fraud. Incidents such as these further drive people into the Internet blog world, which unfortunately can be psychologically detrimental to the individual.

Another series of problems is presented by refined methods of surveillance intruding upon individual privacy. Privacy is after all needed for the individual to search into him- or herself for identity for essential self-development and for relating to others in the real world. Advanced technology and large computer banks owned by both private businesses and government agencies now store enormous amounts of information on each citizen, further alienating the individual from society once he or she becomes a victim.

Society is just now stepping into a technologically upgraded existence with the advent of the mobile phone. The mobile third generation smart phones, such as the Apple iPhone launched in 2007, provide full-featured web access and multimedia capabilities and have a more user-friendly touch screen interface. The increase in web-search requests has touched all search engines such as Google. There have been many more iPhone requests since the iPhone was invented than for any other phones.

The mobile phone is replacing the PC as the primary means of getting online. The individual no longer separates workspace from family space. This new and better technology has caused a social problem. Many users feel over-awed by the opportunities open to them. The office is any place at any time, which increases stress. Anxiety is caused by the fact that people feel they must stay connected to their mobile phone and work even on weekends.

In addition to this, the people sense their aloneness, a disconnection with those around them. Even working in a public area such as a coffee house, the individual excludes him or herself from others who are physically present. He or she is spending social time alone on an iPhone, alienated from the real world.

James Katz at Rutgers University fears that cyber-nomads (as people using their mobile phones are called) are "hollowing out" their third places next in line to homes and offices. They are isolated from the people around them in public spaces that traditionally served as informal social meeting places as they speak on their mobile phones and hack away at their keyboards.

People find themselves not planning, not thinking before writing, and not meeting in what used to be places for physical interaction such as coffee houses or cafes such as Starbucks but rather remaining isolated in their virtual worlds. People lose touch with other individual subjects in society.

II

In analyzing the individual's development of selfhood in the mass consumption and Internet virtual forms of existence, it becomes necessary to discuss the psychological issues of anxiety, alienation, depression, and anomie. In general, in mass culture, the individual loses subject development, which is a distancing of the individual from his or her inner selfhood. The individual becomes an object of dominant forces in society whether they be political or corporate. Advertising is a prime tool. As a result, many people find themselves anxious, alienated or suffering from anomie.

According to Erich Fromm in his book, *The Sane Society*, "the mentally healthy person is the person who lives by love, reason, and faith, who respects life, his own and that of his fellow man. The alienated man... cannot be healthy. Since he experiences himself as a thing, an investment, to be manipulated by himself and by others, he is lacking a sense of self. This lack of self creates deep anxiety.[18]

Fromm states that "mental health, in the humanistic sense, is characterized by the ability to love and to create, by the emergence from the incestuous ties to family and nature, by a sense of identity based on one's experience of self as the subject and agent of one's power, by the grasp of reality inside and outside of ourselves; that is, by the development of objectivity and reason. The aim of life is to live it intensely, to be fully born, to be fully awake."[19]

In American society today, people spend increasingly more time alone on mobile phones and the Internet and far less time with friends in meaningful face-to-face activity. They do not go to the theater for an uplifting and soul-searching experience but seek entertainment as a diversion – to be relieved from thought and reason. They substitute virtual friendships for real ones because virtual friendships are easier to come by. While this avoids conflict and criticism from within the self and from the outside world, it also avoids the search for the truth underlying many of life's fundamental questions.

According to Fromm, the modern person is expected to stand alone by his or her own powers and to reach out of an alienated existence. The individual can achieve a sense of identity only by self-development as a subject.

In other words, the individual must find an existence other than as an object among other objects in society. People must develop their selfhoods. In existentialist terms, the subject self must develop an essence (becoming) out of pure existence (being). That is, the individual must develop a personality with reason and a value system.

The individual must act independently of others. In doing so, he or she must see the world as composed of other active subjects rather than as passive objects for the purpose of manipulation. The real world must be seen as of greater value and importance than the virtual world. Materialistic greed and society's purpose of commercial growth must be dialectically negated in favor of reason, ethics, self-love, and love of mankind.

In society, reform is possible only if the individual develops active powers in relating to the world. In this active world there is a past, present, and future while in the alienated world there is only the present, which the individual conforms to in order to feel secure. In actuality he or she becomes depressed. This is particularly true of those immersed in the virtual world, where the individual exhibits an intense desire to be liked just as others wish to be liked not for the reason of individual differences but for that which makes participants similar despite any personal deviant characteristics.

What is needed is a transformation in mass consumption society away from living to accumulate or to have, to one of seeking to be. The individual must find the courage to be or to exist and to develop his or her selfhood as a subject. In particular, Internet users, who love others as commodities, and who behave as objects to be liked, must change. Developing "aliveness" is infectious in that others will be helped along to transcend egocentricity. With this comes true happiness resulting not from owning, of having more, which only leads to anxiety over longing for more consumer purchases and materialistic relationships but from self-love and subsequent love of others.

Emotional problems exist in mass culture because the psyche of the postmodern individual is such that security is based upon having the approval of one's fellows. Love is an external concept that renders all people equal because it is based upon sex. Happiness, too, is a marketed commodity based upon having fun. Feelings are not active states that result in moral relationships with the outside world. They are products of a passive consciousness that absorbs in a meaningless way from the outside world. The individual acts like an object without free will and proves he or she is a good American by participating in consumption.

The alienated person is an unhappy person, a depressed person. Consumption of fun merely serves to repress an awareness of his or her unhappiness. It avoids the issue. While the subject "I am I" experience can give one the enthusiasm to greet each day as a new experience, the alienated person is only too glad to have finished a day without failure or humiliation.

Conscience is only possible if the individual exists as a subject. Yet, in the postmodern world "mass man" has intelligence that is manipulated. He or she fails to choose among facts. The alienated person is bewildered and willing to elect someone into office if that person offers a total solution. In other words, those seeking office use propaganda to manipulate society, turning democracy into a sham.

The individual who is alienated lives in a state of ethical relativism and conforms to the prevailing attitudes and trends of society. Truth and falsity have no meaning in a thought process like this, which is passive rather than dialectical. While a democracy requires that through reason and debate, citizens determine the best policy alternative for the common good, today language and issues are manipulated by those in political or governmental power. The idea of government by the people is referred to only for propaganda purposes.

In regard to the United States politics and government of today, people are governed by laws, which they do not control. This is an outstanding manifestation of alienation. The state, to which citizens originally delegated authority for representing their interests, now imposes control over them. The individual becomes an object of the "Other," rather than participating in the political process of voicing opinions as an individual or as part of a group of individuals formed to effectuate change.

A problem associated with anxiety and alienation is anomie. Anomie is the state of social instability that results from the breakdown of standards and values. This phenomenon of rootlessness involves a sense of aloneness. It is particularly true of the individual obsessed with the virtual world to the point of losing touch with the real world. People suffering from anomie have no sense of values. They behave as objects of others, trying to emulate others. A product of alienation and anomie is often ennui in the sense of boredom and weariness resulting from having more than enough but wanting more than that anyway in terms of consuming goods and services or wanting more object relationships.

The mass person is rootless in the sense of lacking membership in groups that give meaning to life by providing common purposes and values, shared emotional meanings and relatively fixed roles for the individual to become active in, all of which is essential for democracy to flourish There are no absolutes in regard to morality. Values have deteriorated to a false sense of complacency. The individual has no fixed standards but instead looks for different styles and fashions.

The mass person is socially, intellectually, and spiritually isolated from the ties to the real community. He or she has no standards or values and retreats into a private world such as a virtual world, or seeks to overcome ennui in a constant search for fun. During the early days of the Internet, researchers believed that online experiences were an alternate part of reality. They believed that actions could begin, unfold, and end online without any effect to things off-line.

The fact is that many people are so busy in the virtual world that they forget about the real world. Herein lies the danger of a lack of social development, a disinterest in the functioning of the government, and a disregard for the digression of democracy from its true values. Meaning is lost in terms used by those in power to manipulate the nation state.

The point is that society requires the real world with the bodily presence of persons, and the commanding presence of things. Herein lies the quest for happiness. Any attempt to achieve fulfillment in cyberspace falls far short of the real world and endangers it.

According to philosopher Soren Kierkergaard, to escape the anomie of modernity, the individual needs to form unconditional commitments. This type of commitment establishes 'qualitative distinctions between what is important and what is trivial, what is relevant and what is irrelevant, and what is serious and what is playful' in life, in an effort to determine what has weight in society and its polity. It requires evaluation of reality.

The challenge is to design systems, which integrate online and off-line spheres of action. The problem remains for the individual to be a subject in reality who uses the Internet to facilitate individual and social development in order to control alienation and anomie and the subservice of the individual to those in power who define democracy for their own manipulative purposes. It is only when computer networks facilitate communities oriented toward off-line-oriented action that individuals can gain control of their own existence and essential development as well as the development of society and its polity to reflect the true values of democracy.

III

Granted, the Internet is a fantastic device for obtaining detailed information on countless topics, a problem arises because it has served as a rallying tool for the spread of terrorism around the globe. It has enabled terrorists to recruit members from Columbia to Afghanistan to Thailand with the click of the mouse.

Jihad is an Islamic word is a term denoting anything from an inward spiritual struggle to attain perfect faith to a political or military struggle to further the Islamic cause. It can denote a "holy war." Fighting for Jihad is the highest act jihadists can perform for their cause.

The term 'Jihad' can be used to denote members in the struggle of Islam who become terrorist operatives in groups such as al-Qaeda, which was responsible for the September 11, 2001, bombing of the New York World Trade Center buildings and the Pentagon in Washington, D.C. American intelligence agencies found that then President George W. Bush bolstered terrorism by invading and occupying Iraq. This created a new generation of Islamic radicalism and enhanced the overall global terrorist threat according to the appraisal of different spy services inside the U.S. federal government. Terrorists fight for so-called freedom in Iraq using propaganda against the United States invasion as a rallying cry and the Internet as a tool to spread this terrorist propaganda. Islamic militants no longer have geographic limitations in voicing their Islamic ideology. The propaganda serves to keep individuals as objects in obedience to the terrorists. It also serves the purpose of recruiting new members.

As new Jihadist networks and cells unite, sometimes with little less in common than their anti-Western agendas, worldwide attacks are increasing. In 2006 the independent research group of terrorism experts, called the Council on Global Terrorism, gave a low grade to United States efforts to combat Islamic extremism, concluding that radicalization in the Muslim community is growing and spreading to different parts of the world.

Terrorists can download manuals and videotapes that show them how to make explosive vests, car bombs, chemical weapons and poisons as well as a proliferation of "tips" on how to use them effectively. Some of the newest terrorists are recruited and sometimes trained via the Internet.

A new generation of freelance Web vigilantes has emerged in the past few years. Spending an hour trolling through the Internet postings of Al Qaeda in Iraq, one can find videotapes of smiling suicide bombers affectionately patting their explosives as they prepare to die for their cause and accept their honored place in heaven.

In the face of propaganda, the person informed by the Internet does not reflect upon right or wrong. The individual views the propaganda as the absolute truth, thus he or she no longer exerts a free will to develop an independent opinion of the information being spread. Terrorist propaganda is accepted as having no contradiction to it. As objects, people listening to the propaganda are expected to act rather than first contemplate different alternatives in the quest of what is morally right. It is assumed that the terrorists are "the good." There is no tension between the "is" and the "ought" in this propaganda. There is no subject self-reflection. The United States and the rest of the world are in danger of further terrorist attacks because the Jihadists fight as objects of the Islamic cause.

In the first year after the attacks of September 11, 2001, Congress agreed with the then President G.W. Bush and his Administration that in the name of national security it was necessary to increase the power of the executive branch. After the 9/11 attacks, the Justice Department asked for, and largely received, additional powers that allowed it to perform an unprecedented amount of surveillance of American citizens and visitors. The USA Patriot Act, passed in haste after 9/11, started the ball rolling.

By December 2002, Congress passed two major domestic laws related to the new War on Terrorism and two war resolutions. But, by the beginning of 2003, many members of Congress rebelled against their loss of legislative control and against policies, in particular, the Patriot Act. The Patriot Act was scheduled to desist in 2005, but contrary to Congress's opposition, a second one was passed giving even more power to the executive branch. Public opposition grew.

From the time of the passage of the first act, the public grappled over the problem of balancing national security and protecting civil liberties – freedom of speech, press, religion, and assembly, in particular. This caused a dilemma between the Administration's efforts of rooting out domestic terrorism and Congress's right to be told of these actions, oversee them, and provide funds for them. An encouraging note was that there was a public outcry over the privacy vs. the security issue and the government's right to surveillance. A part of mass society began to awaken. Grassroots activism is on the rise.

Unfortunately, the FBI could secure personal financial information from banks, insurance companies, the U.S. Postal Service, and even jewelry stores and travel agencies without a warrant because they are all construed to be financial institutions. Starting (in 2004), the U.S. government was photographing and fingerprinting foreign visitors coming into this country.

Summarizing polls on privacy over the past fifteen years, it is apparent that few people reported suffering from invasion of privacy by the government in past years, but in recent years, threats to privacy were growing. Many people were afraid that the government would go too far in conducting surveillance and invading their privacy.

This increased public anxiety because of a sense of vulnerability in the light of the fear of terrorist bombing inflicted by the government in justifying the need to sacrifice privacy for the good of the country's security. Under the Bush Administration people felt a sense of alienation and futility as they faced the government's false use of the term democracy to justify surveillance. Individuals felt that they could not influence the government to refrain from excessive control. They felt they could not force the government to return to the people the freedom granted by the Constitution and the laws of the land. Individuals felt alienated as the government enforced an authoritarian arm over their freedom and their right to privacy.

The major features of modern democracy as it should be practiced include individual freedom, which entitles citizens to the liberty and the responsibility to shape their own careers and conduct their own affairs; equality before the law; and universal suffrage and education. This requires protection from violence but not at the excessive infringement of privacy and the force of government authority.

For the government to get information from imprisoned terrorists, or would-be terrorists, torture by means such as waterboarding, or a near drowning experience, was practiced under George W. Bush's Administration. It is certainly possible that the international backlash against torture in the war on terrorism – especially torture that is clearly illegitimate by any defensible criteria, as in Afghanistan and Iraq – led some otherwise friendly countries to refuse to cooperate or to minimize their cooperation with American intelligence efforts. This increased anxiety, alienation and anomie on the part of the public as individuals and as part of the whole society.

Rational and ethical subject citizens are wondering if torture or coercion is morally justified even if the cause is to prevent terrorist attacks in the United

States. Torture was condoned by untrustworthy military and government officials. In the long run, torture can backfire and end by becoming self-defeating as the terrorist cause is given new justification as a result of the suffering imposed on prisoners. In January 2009 President Barack Obama signed an order closing the prison base known for conducting torture in Guantanomo Bay Cuba, a step in the direction of moral responsibility.

Yet, when then President Bush justified torture for national security and the preservation of the American way of life, there was an element in society that felt it was un-American to question the government's actions, be they surveillance or torture. Instead of questioning the difference between democracy as theory and democracy as a slogan to justify undemocratic action, they functioned as objects of government will. Thus, many citizens thought and acted as mass men and women rather than as thinking subjects. They still do today.

"People may respond to exhortations like 'personal responsibility' and 'family values,' but most still expect the government to ensure health care and economic prosperity for them."[20] Deterioration of the situation in Iraq resulted in an implosion of public support for then President Bush and the Republican Party and in a repudiation of Republicans at the polls in the 2006 mid-term elections and the 2008 presidential election. Yet, it seems that the collapse of the Republicans would have been worse had it not been for the expanded and loyal party base and the congressional delegation that Bush and his political strategists fervently cultivated; in other words, support from members of mass society who failed to question the propaganda being imposed or who were part of those doing the imposing.

Although the House of Representatives passed its own non-binding resolution expressing disapproval of the "surge" increase in troops in Iraq, Republicans maintained strong party discipline there, with only 17 members defecting, thus denying the Democrats the rhetorical claim that their resolution represented a bipartisan consensus against the war. Because the Democrats could not secure a vote of "no confidence" against the war strategy, Bush went on the offensive in support of the surge.

Democrats feared that if they did not back the President, it would look as if they did not support the troops. This would spell trouble for the Democratic Party because the public was still an object of propaganda. It believed in the adages of "making the world safe for democracy" and "supporting our fighting men" (and women) risking their lives doing so.

There was an emergence of a government run by one party and the President. This is at the expense of subject individuals aware that United

States democracy guarantees a system of checks and balances and separation of powers, rendering the executive with limited power. The American people suffered acute anxiety due to a high unemployment rate over 10 percent, the stock market seemed unstable trying to slowly recover from a downward spiral, banks faced bad mortgages, and ten of thousands of homeowners faced foreclosures. Companies cut profit forecasts as it became apparent that American consumers in 2008 were facing debts, which stopped them from buying new cars, flat-screen televisions, and other high end consumer products. In the beginning of 2009 the United States faced a deep recession that was probably the main reason that Obama won the presidency.

Mass consumers, who have been programmed to consume, may have to stop buying. They may retreat into the virtual world rather than face the real one of credit card debt and not being able to support the created needs they find unable to live without. Americans are facing the prospect of being forced to live within their means and sending the rest of the world scrambling for buyers with American credit card debt now close to a trillion dollars.

Many economists stated that the economy was in a significant slowdown as housing prices continued to fall, consumer wallets tightened, and businesses cut investments, capital projects, and personnel. This further alienated the individual from the real world and social development and from a democracy that no longer resembled its true meaning.

What is needed is a negation on the part of the individual as a self-being aware of what is wrong with society and its polity, ending in a positive solution. The past, present, and future must be taken into account together with a negation of past wrongs and an affirmation in the present of future possibilities. A negation of mass culture is important whether one lives in affluent times or in times of hardship.

In September 2008, the stock market suffered its worst daily plunge since the September 11, 2001. Financial markets shook because of the sale of Merrill Lynch and the bankruptcy of Lehman Brothers Holdings Inc. The Federal Reserve had to bail out American International Group, the giant insurer and numerous banks. Congress passed and President Bush signed into law a bill allowing the Treasury Department to prop up lenders with a $300 billion stimulus injection, which amounted to a cost of roughly half a trillion taxpayer dollars. This was the largest financial intervention since the 1930's Great Depression and was made in order to keep the financial markets working and to keep the credit freeze from putting the economy into a deep recession. It will take a long time to achieve economic progress again. It remains to be seen what the Obama Administration can do with its costly stimulus packages considering the trillions of dollars national debt it inherited from the Bush Administration.

If consumers cut spending, corporate profits will decline. Granted that, the economy must improve. Rational consumer spending could dampen the massive windfalls – bonuses – that end up in corporate managers' and CEOs' pockets and allow the public, corporate America, and government to spend money rationally and ethically on health care for the needy, affordable higher education, environmental repletion and wild life conservation infrastructure, and much more.

Chapter Five
Selfhood

I

An affirmation of selfhood is required for the individual to make sure that the real world supersedes the virtual and that at the same time the production/consumption process is controlled so that real needs are not confused with irrational desires. Such a revolution of consciousness would insure the use of technology for rational and humane purposes.

The most important factor in changing the direction of culture away from a mass and alienated one to a rational and ethical one is to establish the individual's own control over his or her thought process, so that society and its institutions reflect the individual's will rather than control it. To establish a rational culture in society, conflicts of interest need to be resolved within an ethical framework of the "good," ultimately based upon the self-love of the individual and the love of mankind grounded in the transcendental participation of the self in the Absolute Spirit of love.

When the individual asks, "Who am I?" he or she identifies him – or herself in terms of the organizing principle of personality – selfhood. The individual must love him – or herself first and then others in order to be able to change society for the good.

Just as an individual's existence or being precedes the essential developmental process of becoming what one chooses to be like, so do government and other social institutions exist as a framework for the differentiation of functions to take place in the society composed of individuals. Individuals participate in the input communication of the structural/functional network of governmental policy creation to the extent to which their essential natures are freely developed. In today's United States democratic system, a cultural and economic system based upon the perpetuation of irrationally created wants increases the degree to which individual development is inhibited.

For people to act as free subjects in control of their desires rather than as objects of the production/consumption process, consciousness must be assumed to be superior to nature. It is the subject's responsibility to control technological production and see to it that government reflects the will of the people. The people established their government and can feed it demands in accordance with desired change away from mass culture to a free and ethical one, ensuring that government and the political process function for the good of each individual and society as a whole.

Throughout the centuries of recorded history, social change has occurred when people acting as individuals organize to negotiate grievances and demand change from those elected to serve them through government representation. A subject's awareness of a rational need for change is premised on the truth that consciousness is free and not determined by the false reality of mass culture. While acting as a subject requires subjective thinking, it also requires taking objective circumstances into consideration. The point is that, if free to think, the subject is not controlled by external forces. Once individuals in society act as subjects and as political actors, they are capable of exerting pressure for change.

In the United States today, the insatiable desire for consumer goods has driven more than a million people into bankruptcy each year. People don't save their money. Rather, they borrow to sustain a lifestyle that they feel they must have. A large part of the problem is advertising, which convinces people that they must have what is really just irrational desire fulfillment.

People must use their discretion in choosing what needs and desires should be fulfilled, so that the economy can become a growing and prosperous one, and individuals can save to fulfill true needs and define their own happiness. Mass or crowd behavior must be negated to behavior in which the individual acts rationally to transform him- or herself from existing as an "object" wanting to "have" irrational desires into a subject of rational and ethical thought and action. For example, instead of buying a new boat, an individual could renovate the old one and use the savings to purchase long-term health care insurance on a monthly basis or better home insulation.

On the societal level, individuals as a thinking group of subjects, not as a crowd, can dialectically negate what has happened to democratic values used as propaganda in order to control the unthinking crowd. Values must be reaffirmed to rationally and ethically protect the public according to the original goals that theoretically founded United States democracy.

In general, in mass society people are never satisfied with fulfilling their desires. One desire simply replaces another one that is desired in a long chain of wants. According to William B. Irvine in his book, *On Desire*, as soon as the individual satisfies a desire, he or she experiences psychological adaptation; that is, the individual takes the object for granted and starts feeling dissatisfied. To overcome this feeling, he or she forms a new desire and works to fulfill it.

Irvine explains that if people cannot fulfill the desire they form, they feel dissatisfied, but if able to fulfill felt desires, individuals go on to form new ones, and so remain dissatisfied. What is needed is for the individual to come to realize that there is more to life than simply trying to fulfill created wants.

Success in mass society is much like what Irvine points out. Once "mass man" experience success, he or she recognizes that it feels very good and goes on to set goals just to obtain success for its own sake. After a while it is not so much an object or goal that is important, it is the pursuit itself.

Envy is one of the things that make living with other people difficult. Having success fulfills the desire of being admired, which is one of the prime goals of mass technological society. It is one of the reasons that "mass man" loses him- or herself in the pursuit of success. "For most of us…the choice between worldly success and satisfaction is mutually exclusive. Generally, to gain fame or fortune, a person must be driven by ambition, and a driven person is unlikely to feel satisfied with his circumstances."[1] Individuals lose touch with the core of their beings – their selfhoods – in the sense of not experiencing self-love but experiencing a drive for the pursuit of more, be it an objective pursuit or just the desire for success itself.

On the other hand, with self-love comes satisfaction. It does not matter how wealthy or successful people are. What matters is that they be satisfied with what they have. According to Irvine, it is possible for a person to be both successful and satisfied, but only if what brought the person success also brings satisfaction with it.

For many people, the choice between worldly success and satisfaction is mutually exclusive because an irrational, ambitious drive means that the person is never satisfied. This drive is generally at the root of mass-consumption culture and implies that the individual has not achieved self-love. The individual is in a constant state of discontent rather than in possession of the satisfaction that accompanies self-love.

The enlightened individual has the potential of becoming a master of inconspicuous consumption in comparison to the conspicuous consumption in which "mass man" exists. The conditions of boredom or ennui, anxiety, depression, alienation, and anomie can be overcome if the individual experiences a sense of self-love through an inward projection that connects with the spirit of love.

While Irvine does not consider that ambition pursued with free will can be good for the individual and society, it is true that rational ambition is the cornerstone of social and national progress. Rational progress is "good" progress; it's what moved man out of the cave. The more enlightened society becomes, the more progressive its political system becomes. Success in this light is progress.

People must master desire to break away from irrational consumption of goods that are not real needs but are purchased to such an extent that the future of society is threatened with economic and ecological ruin. Once this is done, the individual is left with a sense of well-being and self-worth. Anxiety can be erased, the environment conserved, and the economy can prosper.

True happiness rather than false consumer happiness is possible because it originates from within the self. The individual no longer suffers from the compulsion to buy, but loves him- or herself and life itself and consumes accordingly.

The key point of the individual's positive development away from mass culture toward self-affirmation is that between ideas and overt acts, there is a state of subjective reflection. Consciousness must be active. A healthy personality adapts to external reality through the effect of the unconscious on the conscious. Dealing with drives and impulses as well as internalized values and prohibitions requires that all parts of the personality balance toward the good. Then, the individual can act to produce rational and ethical change in society and return democracy to the true meaning of its values.

II

C.G. Jung went deeper and further than Sigmund Freud in explaining how the human mind works by introducing the idea that, while there is a personal unconscious in each individual, there is also a collective unconscious. For Jung, the unconscious is not, as Freud believed, entirely unmoral or animal-like nor is it, as some existentialists theorize, a void. It includes moral and even religious principles in the "collective." While the unconscious is partly personal, it is also partly collective, with the collective part going all the way back to include primitive ways of thinking and feeling.

Jung takes a psychological approach, while Freud's standpoint is scientific rather than philosophical. Jung's method is based upon the observation of phenomena such as dreams, myths, and symbols. Through this, Jung deduced that the individual mind is prefigured by evolution. He or she is linked not only to parents and grandparents, but to the entire species before him or her.

Ultimately, he or she inherits from the origins of organic evolution. Jung does not imply that there is no God but rather believes there is ultimately as part of the collective unconscious.

The collective unconscious of the psyche is different from the personal unconscious in that the personal unconscious deals with contents of individual experience, but what is present in the collective unconscious was never part of the individual's conscious lifetime. Just as the body evolves, so does the collective unconscious. It evolves as the brain does.

It is a difficult problem for scientists to explain how a first person subjective experience arises from the neuron-synapse process of the brain. They find the problem hard because no one knows what a solution might look like. In fact, the problem remains a mystery. That is why it is important to understand the psychological analyses of experts such as Jung.

Jung believes that the inherent unconscious drive for human unity exists through the collective unconscious of each individual. Together with the personal unconscious, the root of individual subject being, it results in the thought, will, and the realization of the conscious individual self. This can transform society for "the good" if the individual so wills.

According to Jung, psychologically, all individuals are equal before God, one of the patterns of psychic behavior he termed archetypes, which are always present potentially in the collective unconscious. References to God are in psychological rather than metaphysical terms. Jung does not set out to prove the ultimate cause and nature of mankind but rather the psychological connection between the spiritual God and the individual.

Jung saw the relationship between God and man as a two-way process. Not only does God influence the individual, but also the individual contributes to the conscious reality of God. Jung found that the individual and his or her unconscious self to be in a task of transcendental meaning with God. God becomes more real, the more people believe in Him.

For Jung, only if the individual uses an unprejudiced objectivity – a respect for facts by using reason – can the individual change for the better. Underlying this is spiritual love of the person that is necessary for a transformation, such as that away from mass culture to one based upon ethics. God joins the individual through the self, the archetype whose function is to integrate the various parts of his or her personality.

For Jung, if subjective freedom exists, God appears differently in different cultures and times in a true relationship with subject individuals who determine themselves in light of the relationship between their inner spirits and that of an Absolute Spirit. Jung hoped that the individual could redeem him- or herself of his or her "shadow" or personal evil.

By changing from evil to good, a positive personality based upon self-love develops. Society can function without a dictator or some other form of guardian stepping in to force orders upon the people. In a democracy, which is established by, for, and of the people, individuals assert their selfhood each as one among the many.

In *Modern Man in Search of a Soul,* Jung writes that the spiritual must originate from within the psyche. He points out that, while the West is amazing the East with technological proficiency, it lacks the spiritual insight of the Eastern cultures. The East has a spiritual understanding that confuses the West. Only if individuals participate in a spirit originating from within the psyche can they develop alternatives for action during periods of change and transition. Only through this participation is a change possible from mass culture toward an ethical one.

The basic "wrongness" of Western religious institutionalism is that it does not recognize the question of "good" and "evil," relative to individual experience handed down through the collective unconsciousness. When absolutes set up by churches become dogma instead of doctrine, they merely serve to increase the problem of mental disorder because individuals cannot come to terms with them within their individual experiences. For example, birth control other than abstinence is forbidden by the Catholic Church. This is not feasible for many church goers. In mass culture, the individual has difficulty adapting dogma to personal reality because of the superimposed guilt inflicted by many churches today.

The problem of the individual is to find God within him- or herself and to change society on the basis of this awareness. The dialectical process involved starts with the acceptance of the "shadow"(evil), which must be negated for the good, the two warring halves of the unconscious. At this point these warring halves of the personality reunite, resolved in change for the good as a result of acceptance of the evil. It can be negated at this point. The acceptance and negation process results in changed behavior.

Jung's description resembles the dialectical experience described by the Nineteenth Century religious existentialist Soren Kierkegaard. The resolution in favor of goodness on the personal level results in ethical thought and action in society. Values of freedom, equality, and justice are ultimately based on the goodness found in God.

Unfortunately, when religion becomes dogma, the unconscious no longer has an active role. The inner spirit is dead. This makes obedience to the superstructures of society easier because the critical ability of subjectivity is pacified, rendering the individual an object to be manipulated through the production/consumption process and democracy turned into propaganda for citizens to follow without rational thinking.

In mass culture, religious creed and ritual can be so elaborate and refined that they no longer express the will of the individual. Just as the ideal of democracy congeals into a formality that loses meaning, so the spiritual experience can lose meaning in organized religions. As a result, the individual is alienated from his or her inner self. The individual loses the creativity activated by self-love which is needed to apply doctrine to a personal reality.

In his book, *Transcendent Selfhood*, Yale professor, Louis Dupré, explains that our culture is in a spiritual crisis. He asserts that it is primarily the inner religious experience that determines to what extent the doctrines of organized religions will be accepted. The transcendent ground of consciousness – in which consciousness is both in itself and more than itself – provides the religious feeling in which God is present. Consciousness transcends the objective world to find God in the spiritual.

Dupré states that a meaningful religious experience occurs today only if the center of human piety moves away from external dogma to occur within the self where the individual encounters his or her own transcendence. Mass culture does not provide the individual with a sacred voice. Transcendence can only occur within the inner self.

While in the past religious institutions and their verbal revelations determined the individual's sacred nature, today that is not good enough. It must originate from the inner self-experience, which allows the individual to interpret to what extent doctrine should be accepted. The religious person accepts only doctrine that enhances his or her selfhood.

The philosophy of Søren Kierkegaard is a forerunner of Jung's position. Kierkegaard believed that the individual is not a self-sufficient entity; but rather, that by reflection he or she can discover his or her connection to God. According to Kierkegaard, it is the participation in the perfection of God that gives the individual courage to withstand the aloneness of the individual. Dupré writes in his book, *Kierkegaard As Theologian*, that Kierkegaard believed that a dialectical relationship exists between the subject individual and God that accounts for the individual's own development.

For Kierkegaard, the importance of spiritual participation upon free will is that as a result of the experience, individual ethics are raised to a higher level than that of being man-made. The anxiety and self-doubt accompanying the individual's awareness of his or her fallibility can be overcome because this fallibility no longer determines the framework of choice. Thus, the individual gains the courage to act according to his ethical conviction.

According to theologian Paul Tillich in his book, *The Courage to Be*, the dialectical process in Kierkegaard's theistic existentialism occurs as follows: Individuals, in the presence of God, feel guilt for their sinfulness at the same dialectical moment they feel the forgiveness of their sins by God. The individual's ethical nature depends upon and follows from this experience.

Tillich affirms that faith is the existential acceptance of the transcendental over and above ordinary experience. It is a state of being rather than an opinion. By participating in God, people know that they are affirmed by the power of being itself. In this light, Kierkegaard saw the individual as a category, which in a religious respect, all of mankind must change into from the state of irrational existence. This results in the individual exerting personal responsibility to negate the absurdity of the present crowd culture.

Kierkegaard described a crowd in a manner that relates to the individual in mass society today. He stated that a crowd by its very nature is untruth because it renders the individual irresponsible, or at least weakens his or her sense of responsibility to almost nothing. This is because he or she acts as an object among other objects, none of which are taking any subject responsibility for action.

For mass culture to be transformed into one possessing a meaningful vitality, people must be able to choose their own direction in life. This is necessary for democracy to function. In the climate of apathy, prevalent in today's alienated culture of anomie and ennui, democracy stagnates. In one of irrational patriotism, or mob behavior, the principles of liberty and equality are subject to abuse and manipulation. In the thought process of mass culture, consciousness is passive and reflexive. Individual self-orientation is dictated not by the subject self, but by a superimposed socioeconomic and political order.

In a rational culture, the individual can function on three conscious levels – that of a self-entity in relation to him- or herself and Spirit,(not necessarily the God of established religions), in relation to other subject individuals, and as an object in the objective environment. The subject's conscious existence or being precedes essential development in all activities including material production.

Subject existence is the framework of choice for controlling and changing the essential development of an individual in relation to objective reality. It can lead the individual away from super-imposed subordination and self-gratification in mass-consumption society to viewing the world within a value system based upon ethical reason. An end to the stagnation of mass culture follows. Reality must be examined through a threefold thought process: future action must be contemplated in the present in the context of past experience; this determines how the individual handles present choices for future possibilities for change. Action for the good follows.

The individual must rationally and ethically deal not just with the present "is" but also with the potential "ought" for change. Once the individual subject interprets the present in light of past experience, the dialectical negation of the present passive stagnation of mass culture's reality as false is possible. The thought of potential change can lead to action for an objective change away from mass consumption's irrationally-controlled desires to a future system based upon true human needs and nature.

It is to Jean-Paul Sartre that we owe the existentialists principle that existence precedes essence. People exist before they develop their essential natures. Like Jung, Sartre was concerned with the way the individual plans his or her actions and relates to others as subjects. The danger lies in the person acting as an object without any sense of responsibility. He was concerned with the individual as subject.

According to Sartre, consciousness is based upon the absolute truth that thinking and being are interconnected. For Sartre, the simple truth is that there must be an absolute truth that consists of the individual's sense of his or her own self. While this is contrary to the connection with Spiritual Being, it is because of the importance of the person's thought process as described by Sartre that he is mentioned in this book. His philosophy distinguishes between the individual as a thinking subject and as an object simply absorbing from the external. Individuals become objects in mass culture because they give up their identities to the crowd.

Sartre's aim was to establish the human world as a pattern of values distinct from the material world. Materialism or existing as an object and treating others as objects is no better than existing as an inanimate object like a tree or a table. There is no ability to think subjectively, to change, or to reason. This is true in mass culture of the drive to satisfy desires or of the drive for success for the sole purpose of success.

In dealing with the individual as subject, it is not only the individual him- or herself who is regarded as subject but others as well. Because the rational person thinks, he or she is just as certain of the other person as of him-or-herself. The discovery individuals make in determining their own selfhood reveals to them the selfhood of others as well. Freedom requires that the subject individual necessarily assert him- or herself apart from the material world. It is freedom that allows the individual to think unlike a table, chair, or mass person as an object of mass consumerism and political manipulation.

III

United States democracy has been jeopardized to the extent that "mass man" has lived a passive and alienated existence out of touch with his or her selfhood. In this state the individual is incapable of the critical thinking and self-love needed to preserve democracy and to keep it viable in light of the crises facing it. Democracy has become an object of mass society rather than existing as an ethically active force promoted by subject individuals.

Democracy remains viable only to the point that the individual accepts him- or herself as a self-entity capable of rational judgment and demands factual information from political and economic decision-makers conveyed via undistorted news broadcasting. The individual can then choose the concrete alternatives he or she believes to be morally right and necessary to achieve a just and democratic society.

To change United States democracy from a myth to a reality, individual consciousness must be free to make choices between rational alternatives according to a subjective and pragmatic interpretation of values. The superiority of individual subjective development in connection with objective reality in practice can negate the power of technological manipulation. Objective reality can be organized according to individual choice as long as subject awareness is active, and the individual functions on the basis of free will.

Tantamount to changing society is that the personality of the individual must achieve a state of self-realization. In mass society, the depressive and alienated conditions afflicting many must be overcome with self-love. The loss of principles that the mass person experiences creates a vacuum in the personality that can only be cured by values that arise to take the place of the manipulation imposed from outside of the individual.

People are capable of transforming not only their own lives but by the negation of mass culture they can help align the institutions of American society with democratic principles renewed and rejuvenated. The dialectical conflict between "good" and "evil" can be resolved for the good in the essential development of the self with love. From this arise freedom, equality, and justice for all.

Self-love underlies all that is necessary for free thought, for goodness, and for the democratic values of freedom and equality. There can be no reform of our democratic society unless people establish their own selfhoods on the principle of self-love in its perfect state originating in the Absolute Spirit.

The United States religious heritage, if used rationally, could lead to a more dynamic individual religious experience. Doctrines need not be accepted as dogma. Interpreted with an open mind and applied to personal experience, they could produce a dialectical awakening on the part of the individual. A subjective religious experience could provide individuals with the courage, not only to change themselves but also to change society in accordance with the democratic principles of liberty, equality, and justice. In America's pluralistic society, people need not despair over their own fallibility when faced with divergent opinions if the ultimate source of values, lies in the absoluteness of God, subject to personal interpretation.

Alexis de Tocqueville remarked after his visit to the United States as a young nation, that "it must never be forgotten that religion gave birth to Anglo-American society. In the United States, religion is mingled with all the habits of the nation and all the feelings of patriotism, from which it derives a peculiar force."[2]

Chapter Six
Exercising Values

I

In a democracy, along with granting the individual fundamental freedoms such as speech, press, religion, and assembly, the government calls on the individual to act with self-restraint to protect the freedoms and the equality of all others. In theory, civil liberties are protected in the United States through the Constitution and federal, state, and local laws so that no single group or individual has the political power to curtail the rights of others. Democracy is realized when individual subject beings function and interact in society to influence the outcome of government policies for all through a demand structure that is accessible to all.

The democratic system of government in the United States began with a process of authority derived from the approval of the people. The Constitution is a living document describing how the government represents the will of the people. There is no limit to citizen control or competency. The Revolutionary War changed the hands of those exerting authority to reflect different social and political demands, yet a basic order remained. The citizens developed a subject awareness that their role politically was to maintain control of the governmental *structural/functional* process.

For the individual to question the legitimacy of the government assumes that he or she has the choice open to change what he or she considers to be wrong with the functioning of politics and the government. The choice is not only given to the individual by the laws of the state and the norms of society but ultimately by the critical ability of each person's own consciousness. In theory, control over the functioning of government is ultimately derived from the consent of the people.

It is the job of each of us to see that power is not used as power for power's sake but to serve as authority to preserve liberty, equality, justice, and reason for all, and to further the better existence of man and woman kind. Political authority must not serve to increase the riches of a few at the expense of others but to protect the whole of society from poverty and to allow those who can to use moral means to better themselves over others while protecting the rights of all. It is the job of each individual to insure that liberty, equality, and justice are being practiced by the government for one and for all.

In the United States change is possible because people are prone toward believing they can work together. The belief in the cooperativeness and trustworthiness of people increases the political activity of an individual. A corollary to this is that if individuals have a positive opinion of their fellow individuals, they are more likely to try to effectuate change that will humanly benefit everyone. This attitude reflects a concern for the future of mankind's economic prosperity and at the same time for conserving the environment for future use. It occurs when the individual reestablishes a connection with his or her selfhood to assert a love of the self that extends to a love of others, a belief in the goodness of others, and a desire to perpetuate society and its environment in accordance with an ethical and rational framework originating from within the self.

Furthermore, in our democratic system, the structure of political activity potentially invites open conflict so that all tension and hostility is vented at the same time that compromise and change are put into practice. Individuals become aware of the need for action to defy mass culture's falsehood and subsequent alienation and anomie while preserving the political framework that makes change possible.

Thus, effective change away from a mass culture to a rational and ethical one can result in converting ideas into political demands that can change the socioeconomic system. Violent opposition is not likely to destroy the political process. It is expected that citizens not only express opinions and grievances but obey laws and policy output as well. The structure of the political system provides the means to settle grievances without violence.

Those in government office should be responsive to demands made. Thus, there tends to be less need to rely on force in maintaining order. This is the ideal for changing a culture from perpetuating irrational desires and production into one stimulating rational and ethical decision-making. It depends upon each individual with personal desires and needs to act as part of the collective for the good of each person and the good of the common social network. Compromise may be necessary in the pursuit of individual goals.

Gabriel A. Almond and Sidney Verba in their book, *The Civic Culture*, describe the political form of democracy through a *structural/functional* analysis in which the cultural role characteristics of citizens in the political state are discussed. If United States democracy is to be realized within the scope of a rational civic culture, the citizen as political participant must be able to determine if public policy and political proposals comply with the values and needs of a democratic society including a rational national security.

Conflicts of interest must be resolved according to a principle of justice based upon truth and the liberty and equality of each member of the political community. Compromise must be arrived at within the range of rational choices in the interest of economic and political justice for all.

Competent citizens exert political influence if they have an awareness of their political effectiveness. In the United States, formal organizations such as political parties, trade unions, and churches are very important to the political process. They aggregate individual demands and communicate them to the government. Also, informal social groups, such as work groups, senior citizens, and neighbors, communicate demands to the various levels of government and play a role in communicating the influence government has upon the individual to the individual. The Internet can play a major positive role in facilitating this communication process. Different demands made upon the government through the political process can result in policies that will change mass culture into a rational one.

Individuals, formal organizations, and informal groups can exert influence on the institutions of society such as that of the media by complaints, protests, as well as support. Change is inevitable. But, of course, first there must be a change within the individual. Reform of churches can prove to be invaluable in this regard by reinforcing the message of a connection between selfhood and God on a personal basis and giving the public ethical values to reform society's institutions. In essence, the individual's selfhood must be developed in such a way that a perception of a political role is included. The individual's political actions follow from the conscious determination of such a purpose.

Because democracy requires a sense of brotherhood and sisterhood as well as community spirit of its people, it is important for the individual to participate at least marginally in cultural and community affairs and organizations. It is the individual, alone or part of a group, who is the center of cultural and social affairs because of the absence of hereditary or arbitrary class distinctions determining political power.

Participation ensures the vitality of democracy. It ensures political representation of the common interests expressed by individuals alone or part of a group. It must be remembered that in a democracy there is power in numbers. The majority rules in the United States political system with the minority potentially becoming a majority.

Almond and Verba describe the community organization that fosters effective and stable democracy as follows: There is political activity but not so much that governmental authority is destroyed; there is moderate involvement and commitment; there is political cleavage that is kept in check. The United States government and social systems are held together by mutual trust among different cultures and social existences. It is this that keeps the country moving together in times of strife and disagreement.

Individuals must realize that through their selfhood, they can control their destiny. They can defend and promote their individual and collective liberty and equality both politically and economically. They can and must liberate themselves from mass culture and its institutions. Democracy is not a spectator sport but rather a participatory process.

In the United States democratic system the structure of political activity invites open conflict so that all tension and hostility is vented at the same time that compromise toward change is achieved. Thus, effective change away from the irrational culture of non-representative policies toward a rational one supporting ethical democracy can result in converting ideas into political demands that change socio-economic and political circumstances to reflect democratic values.

Reform is tempered by compromise and compliance on the part of individuals with active free wills. Those holding government office are expected to be responsive to public demands. Responsiveness to demands maintains order. Functioning is based upon the input-output structure. Policy demands are followed by policy formation or adjudication, which in turn results in new demands and support made upon the political/governmental structure.

In formulating policy, government decision-making must be based upon sound experience and rational, pragmatic judgment applied to specific issues and problems raised by citizen support and demands. Once policy is determined, the government bureaucracy should be organized, so that policies and programs are implemented with a view toward a proposed long-term effect. Policy output then influences public support for the political-governmental process.

United States democracy, established to protect individual rights within the context of the common good, takes into consideration both economic and political rights because "happiness" depends upon both. The laws of this nation must incorporate the ideals of liberty and equality for the purpose of achieving a just and viable political community. The individual's right to pursue his or her own happiness is protected as long as he or she does not infringe upon the rights of others.

Our republican democracy is one in which the wants of the American people should be made part of and should be respected by the government. "The normative requirements are: First, that there be institutions and procedures that facilitate control by the American people, which can be called 'procedural' or 'institutional' democracy; ...second, that there be recognizable representation of the people in what government does, which can be referred to as 'substantive' democracy; ...and third, that there be vigorous protections of the individual rights and liberties of the people."[1]

The legislative, executive, and the judicial systems in this country, on all levels of government, form and determine policies and laws. Through rules and procedures the American voters hold political leaders accountable. Furthermore, public opinion has a role in government policy making. This is what can be referred to as substantive democracy.

Theoretically, in a democracy all government decision-making is based upon the consent of free and equal citizens in society. It is based upon individual awareness of political effectiveness. The pervasiveness of mass culture today requires a reexamination of the principles of liberty, equality, and justice to determine how far American society has digressed from functioning according to the true meaning of these values. Through a dialectical awakening this would allow United States citizens and their elected officials to reapply those principles to reality for the purpose of reestablishing an ethical democracy.

II

A contemporary interpretation of liberty, equality, and justice can be found in Mortimer J. Adler's book, *Six Great Ideas*. Adler states that the foundation of "inalienable liberty" is in the natural possession all people have of free will. He believes that society provides us with the freedom to do as we please within the constraints of justice and the political liberty granted to the enfranchised.

In the United States, laws theoretically protect the liberty and equality of citizens by the common consent of the people. The government's role is to provide for a redress of grievances according to the principles of liberty, equality, and justice based upon truth, and to ensure the favorable conditions necessary for citizens to secure their own happiness.

A deprivation of political freedom – liberty – would make it impossible for the individual to participate in political affairs to protect his or her inalienable rights and to pursue his or her own happiness according to a personal interpretation of it. Americans are denied political freedom when they are denied citizenship or when they are refused the rights of citizenship (most fundamentally, the right to vote), even though they are citizens as was true of women until the Nineteenth Amendment to the Constitution.

Adler states in regard to equality that justice does not deal with personal equality, referring to the attributes we are born with or acquire during our lifetime. Instead, justice deals only with equality that is circumstantial; that is, the right to do as we please by virtue of the fact that we are all human. Thus, the Constitution, federal, state, and local laws must protect the equality of all United States citizens according to a nondiscriminatory practice.

Justice prescribes that all individuals are entitled to circumstantial equality "in kind" especially with respect to economic status, treatment, and opportunity because everyone is human. Adler states, "being by nature equal, (we) are all endowed by nature with certain unalienable rights, unalienable because they are inherent in man's specific nature, not merely bestowed upon man by legal enactment. Legal enactment may be necessary to secure these rights, but it does not constitute their unalienability."[2] Unalienability is a given.

The *Declaration of Independence* states: "We hold these truths to be self-evident, that all men are created equal; that they are endowed by their Creator with certain inalienable rights; that among these, are life, liberty and the pursuit of happiness." The next sentence defines the function of government (and by implication, laws) as "to secure these rights governments are instituted among men."[3] According to Adler:

> "Just as all human beings are entitled to a political equality in kind, so they are all entitled to an economic equality in kind. All should be haves with respect to political liberty, none have-nots, none disenfranchised persons totally deprived of the power of political participation that a political animal needs. All should be haves with respect to wealth in the form of whatever economic goods a human being needs to live well, at least that sufficiency of such goods which is enough for the purpose. None can be have-nots in the sense of being totally deprived of such goods, for total deprivation means death. But none should be destitute – have-nots in the sense of being deprived of enough wealth to live well."[4]

These concepts of liberty and equality are humane and should have been in effect from the beginning of United States nationhood. However, as with most principles, they have required time to broaden in application to conform reality to the ideal. The American Indian, women in general, and African Americans among others have been denied equality under the law from the beginning of nationhood. Inroads to correcting these injustices have been slow in coming. In the case of African Americans, it took the Civil War just to end slavery. Justice requires that basic needs encompass more than what is needed for survival. It must provide for a decent life-style for everyone to live in relative comfort.

The United States political and judicial systems have in the past had to amend practices that have denied American citizens their inalienable rights to liberty and equality before the law. The political and judicial systems have been used time and time again by individuals seeking redress of their grievances.

It is important to add that Adler's principles must apply to rational applications of liberty and equality in kind and in degree and not in terms of uncontrollable wants and desires termed needs by those who are apt to gain by such an application to the political, governmental, and market systems. Justice requires that although all citizens must be granted equality "in kind," they need not all possess equality "in degree." Justice grants more to some and less to others in terms of equality in degree. For example, while all citizens have political power via their right to vote, those holding government office have more power because they are responsible for enacting and implementing laws in light of a political mandate granted them by the popular vote and in the case of the presidency by electoral vote.

Justice entitles some who have to have more than others and some to have less in varying degrees, as long as no one is granted so much that others do not have enough for their livelihood. This is in regard to rational pursuits both referring to political and economic goals.

In American society today, citizens must make the effort needed to ensure that their elected representatives vote according to their demands rather than according to the influence of powerful vested interests, such as the oil conglomerates – especially if the American public is suffering as a result, for example, from higher prices for gasoline to fuel automobiles and for food to put on the table.

People must have enough resources to allow them to live well – above the level of subsistence. All people must have sufficient economic resources available to them to satisfy their real needs based upon rational judgment.

They are entitled not only to equality of opportunity but to equality of conditions needed to make them all equal in kind. This equality in kind consists of health, knowledge, and leisure because by current standards, these factors constitute a "good life." Leisure-time activity enables individuals to pursue personal fulfillment rationally determined for their own happiness. For example, a day at the beach to enjoy a swim with someone is rational, while going into debt to buy a swimming pool to keep up with or surpass the one a neighbor has is irrational.

Democracy does not equate economic liberty and equality with political liberty and equality, which should determine the practice of the former. While ethical democracy does not preclude capitalism, it does require that capitalism conform to its basic principles of liberty and equality in the interest of humanity – subject to political interpretation by free and equal citizens and their elected representatives.

While some people may contribute more to the economic progress of the United States through their skill, intelligence, and hard work, they are entitled only to their fair share of equality in degree over the economic equality in kind necessary for each person in society to live decently. This puts a ceiling on the irrational desires of mass culture, which accompany false needs or desires, and greed and corruption in the name of the "American dream."

In the name of democracy, it is the duty of citizens to help determine what services should be provided for the public and how much of the national budget should be allocated for defense purposes instead of social services. Individuals alone or as part of associational and non-associational interest groups need to exert a rational political voice against the depletion of financial and natural resources not only for their own benefit but also to promote peace and cooperation between the United States and other nations.

For citizens to secure political equality and voter strength, they must first become aware of the discrepancy between democracy's ethical nature and the reality of its practice. Individual citizens realize their potential political power to change public policy so that it conforms to democratic principles.

Voter strength could provide elected officials with the mandate needed to enact and enforce rational policy and programs accordingly, especially in local political-governmental affairs where citizens can effectuate control easiest. Important, however, is participation in the general election of the President of the United States because of the individual's actual and perceived powers. In November 2008 Barack Obama won the presidential election with a mandate for change because people expressed their desire for change rationally through the vote, which was a statement of political equality in kind.

If each individual is to be free to pursue happiness within the context of the common good, government must ensure economic freedom and equality in kind for all. The standards for determining what constitutes these rights are defined by economic conditions and by a humane and rational interpretation by each citizen, exerting a political vote.

While Adler deals with the rights of citizens, it is important to note that non-citizens should also be entitled to basic rights by virtue of the fact that they are human. Otherwise, they may never be able to become citizens. For example, all individuals should be entitled to a life-style above subsistence and a fair chance to become citizens.

Furthermore, we are facing an energy crisis today. There is a shortage of what we are dependent upon. It is up to each individual in society to determine which energy resources to tap now and in the future and, in general, for what purposes. The goal is not to control nature but to control the social forces that irrationally abuse nature.

Writing in the late 1950s in his well-known book, *The Affluent Society*, John Kenneth Galbraith offered the following solution that can be applied today for obtaining needed public funds to assist in providing for economic equality in kind and in degree and protecting the environment:

> "…a system of taxation which automatically makes a *pro rata* share of increasing income available to public authority for public purposes. The task of public authority like that of private individuals, will be to distribute this increase in accordance with relative need. Schools and roads will no longer be at a disadvantage as compared with auto- mobiles and television sets in having to prove absolute justification."[5]

This would reverse the cultural trend away from wasteful demand-creation and mass consumption of created desires toward one that humanely provides for the essential needs of the people. Because the market is imperfect, the government should also introduce economic techniques such as loose price ceilings on selected goods, eliminate particular price floors and regulate selected industries for the benefit of society as a whole. It is not anti-capitalist to insist that United States democracy provide a decent life-style for all its citizens. Rather, it is simply inherent in the ethical nature of democracy that it not be linked to any one economic system, but that whatever system adopted (in the American case, capitalism) take into consideration the liberty and equality of the people.

Democracy as a political process must see that technology works to protect and advance people and their environment. The United States economy requires pragmatic government intervention on the basis of democratic values to provide for a rational distribution of income that protects all individuals in society. This does not prevent those who are capable of successful competition from obtaining economic "equality in degree." It merely ensures that all others are not deprived of their "equality in kind."

Individuals working together in the United States can dialectically interpret and reinterpret democratic principles as circumstances change to achieve a higher synthesis of ethical values with economic and political conditions. It is possible, though not inevitable, to have a dialectical progression toward a "perfect" democracy – a political community basing its existence upon the rational and pragmatic interpretation of democratic principles, perhaps including abandoning the electoral college system to allow for the popular election of the president and leaving the selection of the vice-presidential candidates up to the voters.

Learning from past mistakes in the present can lead to a more "perfect" democracy in the future. The dialectical progression requires a sublimated vision of what "could be" for actual change to occur.

III

The American people in recent years suffered greatly from irrational manipulation and a lack of political representation compounded by false media coverage. The public was denied liberty in kind and degree. Inaccurate media coverage of the facts related to the nation's most important issues limited the possibilities for fully enlightened political engagement by the public. This compounded the problem associated with the Iraq War in which Congress abdicated its war powers. In practice, "the executive branch is allowed to monopolize information and go unchallenged in its justifications for its actions"[6] relating to involvement in the war.

In regard to the Iraq War, public opinion was manipulated by public relations firms. The nation's press did not protect the American people from this manipulation. U.S. foreign policy was undemocratic because President Bush and his aides misinformed the public in a way that led it and Congress to misperceive the national interest in terms of going to war.

The public was led to fear that Iraq had chemical, biological, or nuclear weapons of mass destruction.

Confused about how to present the war and gain support for it, the Administration emphasized the threat to national security. Thus, public support was gained by misrepresentation, since it was never proven that these weapons existed and then later determined that such weapons never did exist. Congress was to blame, too, by the fact that it gave the President unchecked power in deciding to go to war. Also there was never a proven connection between Saddam Hussein and the terrorists of al Qaeda as the President and the media proclaimed.

Through propaganda, the public was denied its fundamental political right or equality in kind to exert influence regarding participation in the Iraq War. True knowledge of the circumstances of involvement was denied. Citizens could not determine for themselves if the war was justifiable or not.

The press failed to enlighten the public about the falsehood underlying involvement in Iraq. The Bush administration attempted to manipulate, if not mislead, the public via a public relations campaign that included government-supported news reports for broadcast on local television stations. It is difficult for people to present their views and petition the government if the press does not present the facts correctly and truthfully to them.

This raises the issue of protection of rights and liberties for each individual in America. It raises the issues of how individuals can practice the right to vote – a right in kind – to influence the government to rationally represent their interests according to the values underlying United States democracy. "The government's response to the terrorist attacks of September 11, 2001 and its initiation of war in Iraq have drawn renewed attention to the separation of Congress' power to *declare* war from the president's power to *conduct* war as commander in chief.[7]

"The Iraq Study Group Report" of 2006, co-chaired by James A. Baker, III and Lee H. Hamilton requested unity on the part of the American people. It requested a bipartisan approach to the conclusion of the Iraq War and support by the people. As history testifies, President Bush ignored the report.

Two other threats to American democracy were "the mean-spiritedness that has come with partisan conflict and the religious intrusion into contemporary politics."[8] First, there was former House of Representatives Majority Leader Tom DeLay's response to investigations of his own behavior and to attacks by Democrats, as well as the zeal with which he wanted Congress to alter the way the courts act as institutions, thereby threatening to undermine the role of the judiciary in the separation-of-powers system. Second, the religious fervor seen in the efforts to keep the brain-dead woman, Terri Schiavo, on life support from 1990 to March 31, 2005 – at odds with medical experts, her husband, and public opinion –added to turn both incidents into an incendiary combination.

This raised serious questions about the fundamental political right of citizens to vote and of the nature of majority rule in the United States. What the public needs is responsible parties that present it with clear choices for which they are held responsible at election time rather than to lose themselves in an irrational brawl pitting political parties against each other and infusing religious fervor into what should never have been raised considering the principle of the separation of church and state.

As a result of these and other issues, there was an awakening on the part of the American people. What has developed was a growth of grassroots political activity on the part of average American individuals. Jerome Armstrong and Markos Moulitsas Zuniga proclaim in their book, *Crashing the Gate*, that the reformation was underway. "A whole new generation of progressive activists has stepped in to engage the fight against the conservative juggernaut."[91] The Internet provided for grassroots activity, termed by Armstrong and Zuniga as netroots activity. It resulted in people communicating via Internet blogs in an effort to reform the political system. For the first time in decades, people took hold of their own destiny. Of issue was the following:

> "Republicans have convinced some of these poorest of the poor that government is powerless to improve their economic situation, so they focus on "values" issues instead: Terri Schiavo, abortion, gays, prayer in the school, the *Ten Commandments* in public spaces...."

(Included in this, of course, was the attempt to ward off the "Axis of Evil "in the Middle East and the slogan "to make the world safe for democracy.")

> "The promotion of these values becomes the government's top concern, even as the economy suffers and war rages."[10]

Citizens fought back for economic reform and against wars that did not reflect citizen consent. The public became aware of the fact that democratic values were misinterpreted by the government to gain support for policies that are contrary to the public good. People fought back with pragmatic efforts to end this falsehood by instituting change. The sum total of individuals fighting for their own well-being for themselves and others came to the fore on the horizon. The original values of liberty, equality, and justice were not being overlooked but were being fought for pragmatically to secure a decent lifestyle for all. Hopefully, people who truly represented the public were being elected to office.

Grassroots and netroots activities were providing for democratic participation from real people. They were combining the real world with the virtual world. This real activity is one solution to the current problems of anomie and alienation partly caused by the absorption of individuals in the virtual world away from the real one.

Political consultants in some cases used advertising to appeal to a rational society, one not connected to mass culture, which promotes subject development and the true values of democracy. Rational and ethical thinking must be at the basis of a candidate's campaign. Consultants must keep this in mind. Advertising can be used to inform people as to what is available for maintaining a good life and a political system based upon reason and ethics.

If netroots combines with grassroots to inspire people to campaign out of love for mankind and its environment with the principles of equality in kind and degree for all, then the falsehood of mass culture's political and economic systems can gradually be eliminated.

Statistically, young people are less likely to vote than their older American counterparts. Yet, youth participation, which began to increase in 2004, greatly increased in 2008. It is everyone's responsibility to see that democracy is reborn for each coming generation. Many citizens who never involved themselves in politics did in 2008. This is necessary to prove that democracy is not dead and that people are inherently good. Perhaps this was a period of creedal passion.

Conclusion
Where We Go Now

The purpose of this book has been to point out the extent to which United States democracy practiced for the past decades has been and still is a myth, and to present the possibility for change through the ethical and rational development of the individual and his or her subsequent political action for reform.

Its other purpose has been to offer an alternative to the irrational consumer culture that occupies most of America's thinking today. The individual need not suffer alienation, anomie, and the accompanying depression and anxiety that afflict so many of us. While these maladies are not always the fault of our culture, the irrationality of mass consumption culture is a prime factor. The development of selfhood through love and understanding benefits not only the individual, but also society as a whole and its democracy.

Democracy can become a reality only if people rationally and pragmatically interpret its meaning based upon the principles of liberty, equality, and justice for all. Citizens, especially those entrusted with political office, must accept a personal responsibility for determining rational public policy alternatives according to democratic principles.

U.S. democracy requires that political and governmental decision-making be based upon the statement found in the *Declaration of Independence* that "all men are created equal; that they are endowed by their Creator with certain inalienable rights; that among these, are life, liberty, and the pursuit of happiness." By turning ideals into reality today, this should spill over to all people and not just citizens. This requires adherence to the accepted principles of freedom, equality, and justice in political and economic terms, interpreted and reinterpreted as societal change warrant. The individual must be protected in the pursuit of happiness.

"Happiness consists in our touching the rock bottom of reality, in the discovery of our self and our oneness with others as well as our difference from them. Happiness is a state of intense inner activity and the experience of the increasing vital energy, which occurs in productive relatedness to the world and to ourselves."[1] It cannot be found in mass culture, which is responsible for passive and alienated individuals. The happy person is the internally fulfilled person not the person who is superficially empty and constantly trying to be satisfied.

All United States citizens are entitled to political liberty and equality to protect themselves and their "pursuit of happiness" within the political community; they are entitled to economic liberty and equality so that they can live decent lives. Beyond this, they are entitled to more political liberty according to their increased political responsibilities, such as holding office and to more wealth according to their success at competing for it. This requires a humane interpretation of free enterprise and capitalist accumulation, which makes it subject to qualification by the democratic political process in the interest of both the common good and individual freedom.

Democracy requires that government decision-making be based upon the consent of the governed as free and equal citizens of the political community. Unfortunately, throughout American history certain segments of society have accumulated too much political and economic power at the expense of the whole of society or parts of it. And let us not forget noncitizens.

However, active coordination on the part of individuals seeking change, helped by responsible government representatives and leaders making rational, principled decisions, can result in reform in the interest of freedom, equality, and justice. The key point is that between ideas and overt action, there is a state of subjective reflection in which individuals critically determine the rightness or wrongness of objective circumstances. This leads to action for reform.

Encouraging today, in regard to the practice of ethical democracy, is the fact that individuals have joined action groups both in terms of grassroots and netroots with goals centering upon public control of the government and the economy. Netroots is an example of how the Internet and other information and communication technologies can be used to broaden and deepen citizen engagement and enhance democratic deliberation.

Technology can change the capacities of different groups through communication and organization. There has been a new progressive movement trying to give more control to the rank-and-file Americans who need a larger voice in controlling the government and the economy.

Democracy's use value lies in providing an ethical focal point for individuals with critical minds to use in transforming government by the few, reversing a failing economy, and reforming mass-consumption culture according to specific reform objectives. Democracy creates an environment of freedom that enables the individual to shape his or her own essential development, hopefully within a framework of reason and morality.

Individuals, making choices together between the options offered by competing political parties on the basis of a shared concept of democracy, can help determine economic priorities that reduce the nation's unemployment rate, equalize income distribution, and eventually control the size of the national deficit as well as the allocation of the budget. Of course, these reforms require rational and ethical choices on the part of the people and their parties. It is the responsibility of concerned citizens and political aspirants to ensure that these choices are available to all.

A consensus is possible on democratic value interpretation, not only because individuals in American society share similar experiences, but also on the basis of the internalization of all human experiences in the collective unconscious described by C.G. Jung. The individual not only shapes his or her essential nature in the present, but also has the accumulated experiences of all of mankind active in his or her collective unconscious.

Herbert Marcuse in his book, *One-Dimensional Man*, states that in mass culture the human mind is pacified into a passive thought pattern. The destruction of individual will and creative thought is accepted because of the satisfaction gained by participation in mass consumption. This self-indulgence in consumption is enhanced by the false application of technology to further control consciousness. Marcuse states that the range of choice open to the individual does not decide his or her degree of freedom. Free choice among a wide variety of goods and services does not provide freedom if these goods and services foster a life of fear and alienation.

What is required for an alternative existence to mass pacification and its subsequent maladies is a reevaluation of existence on the basis of self-love. This leads to a reinterpretation of needs, not on the basis of superimposed desires and the means to satisfy these desires, but upon what is essential not only for existence but also in terms of what makes the individual truly happy. People must treat each other on the basis of being subject beings rather than as objects to be manipulated to fulfill irrational desires. One positive sign is that there is a growing awareness that leaders in corporate American must possess the quality of reason rather than just intelligence.

What each of us is faced with is that the economy is in trouble. Just two generations ago, Americans were living within their means and putting some money aside in savings. In 2008 Americans carried over two trillion dollars in consumer debt according to the Federal Reserve Board.

But, consumers are starting to overcome their sense of alienation. They are voicing their anger over lending practices. When the Federal Reserve Board drafted a proposal against abusive practices faced by borrowers, it received a massive number of letters from people who had suffered from these unfair lending practices. Consumers are taking action.

Irrational spending is being forced to decline because of economic hardship. American consumers are increasingly reluctant to spend. They fear what will happen to them if they run out of money, since the economy is only recently showing signs of an upswing out of the deep recession it is in. Employment is in a precarious state. If businesses reduce personnel or shut down completely, money will not be flowing freely.

Many consumers cannot spend money on luxury items but need it for food and fuel. With disposable income strained by rising prices, people traveled less and cut back on purchases of clothing and electronics. Mid-range and luxury retail chains were forced to postpone or cancel expansion plans because of the cut in consumer spending. It would be better if the economy were expanding, people were given the choice of rational spending, and they took it.

Nevertheless, it is apparent that profligate spending habits are unlikely to return soon. All of this puts a damper on mass culture. While the economy has forced people to cut back before, it is necessary this time for individuals to refute their spending practices of the past and seek rational alternatives for the reform of a future based on present possibilities. The individual must learn from the past how not to define him-or-herself in terms of being a commodity to be exploited.

Assuming that only a fundamental change in human nature from a "having" to a "being" mode of existence can reform society and save individuals from a psychological and economic catastrophe, the question arises: Is large-scale personality change possible and, if so, how can it be brought about?

The following conditions must exist: 1) We must face that we are suffering from alienation and anomie; 2) We must recognize that the origin of our ill-being is derived from mass culture – that is, from irrational demand creation for products and policies superimposed by advertising, the media, and the political and economic hierarchy in control of our society; 3) We must recognize that there is a way of overcoming our problems by practicing our selfhood of love and rational thinking; and 4) We must accept that to overcome our existence in mass culture we must follow our rational and ethical values as stated in the U.S. Constitution.

These four points correspond to the *Four Noble Truths* that form the basis of the Buddha's teaching dealing with the general condition of human existence. The function of a new existence and that of a new democratic society relies on the emergence of new individuals whose character structure will exhibit the following qualities:

"Willingness to give up all forms of having in order to fully be.

Security, sense of identity, and confidence based upon faith in what one is, on one's need for relatedness, interest, love, solidarity with the world around one, instead of on one's desire to have, to possess, to control the world, and thus become the slave of one's possessions.

Developing one's capacity for love, together with one's capacity for critical, unsentimental thought.

Making the full growth of oneself and of one's fellow beings the supreme goal of living.

Knowing that to reach this goal, discipline and respect for reality are necessary.

Developing one's imagination, not as an escape from intolerable circumstances but as the anticipation of real possibilities, as a means to do away with intolerable circumstances.

Sensing one's oneness with all life, hence giving up the aim of conquering nature, subduing it, exploiting it, raping it, destroying it, but trying, rather, to understand and cooperate with nature.

Freedom that is not arbitrariness but the possibility to be oneself, not as a bundle of greedy desires, but as delicately balanced structure that at any moment is confronted with the alternative of growth or decay, life or death.

Control of the Internet rather than being controlled by it.

Politically becoming part of grassroots/netroots activity out of self-love and love of humanity and U.S. democracy.

Most of all remembering that happiness is the process of ever growing aliveness, whatever the furthest point is that fate permits one to reach, for living as fully as one can is so satisfactory that the concern for what one might or might not attain has little chance to develop."[2]

In mass-consumption culture, the institutions of government and society reflect an irrational will rather than a rational thought process. Order is maintained by responding to this irrational demand creation. The reward is the self-perpetuation of the system. Thus, the primary function of government is to keep the socio-economic system running to the tune of irrational consumption and one-dimensional or passive thought.

For a change to occur, individuals working collectively in society must negate irrationality and center upon the self in control of wants and needs. The political process must reflect this change in the communication input and output of the decision-making policies of government.

In the United States people work together for change. Because people trust and cooperate with each other, the political activity of each person existing under the country's democracy increases. If individuals have a positive opinion of their fellow Americans, they are more likely to effectuate change that will humanely benefit everyone. This attitude reflects a concern for the future of mankind for political change and conserving the environment for future generations.

The United States democracy has a structure of political activity that invites open conflict, so that all tension and hostility are vented at the same time that compromise and change are put into practice. Thus, effective reform away from mass-consumption culture to a rational one can result in converting ideas into political demands that can change the socioeconomic system. Violent opposition does not destroy the political process. It is a tradition that citizens not only express opinions and grievances but obey laws and policy output as well.

Those in government office are expected to be responsive to demands made. Thus, there is no need to rely on force for maintaining order. Changing a culture from perpetuating irrational desires to rational and ethical decision-making is thus possible.

Our patriotism determines our perception of our responsibilities as citizens. There have always been two different types of patriotism in American history. The first is based upon what we have achieved. The second looks to our future and how we live up to what we believe makes up our greatness. Conservatives and liberals argue about which definition is the correct one. What we need is a type of patriotism that combines the two for the best decisions we can make in the present, using the results of the past, to determine the best outcome for the future.

The Founding Fathers did not envision the conditions of American culture and society as they are today when they drafted the Declaration of Independence. Yet, democracy has more to offer United States citizens and those wanting to become citizens, now than ever before. Technology can add to the wealth of present and future generations so that political and economic liberty in kind and in degree can be realized to a far greater extent than ever before.

United States citizens have a vast number of choices open today as a result of technological advances and innovation. Scientific and medical discoveries can be used to preserve and protect humanity and the environment. The possibility and opportunity exist to adequately take care of the real needs of all members of society as well as to provide assistance where and when it is needed and requested around the globe.

Ultimately, it is up to each individual to transform United States democracy from a myth into a reality. As Paul Tillich states in his book, *The Courage to Be*, "The courage to be as oneself is the courage to follow reason and to defy irrational authority."[3] This requires freedom – our gift for being part of the United States democratic system.

Epilogue

Today, in the beginning of the second year of the presidency of Barack Obama, the United States must strive for change if its democracy is to one day represent the freedom, justice, and equality it should represent. Rational and ethical responsibilities must be met.

It is this author's opinion that President Obama is a president of the people despite bank and automaker bailouts that increased the deficit and cost taxpayers money. After all, what was owed has been repaid to the Treasury Department by the automakers.

President Obama laid a new foundation for economic growth in his first year in office, warning us that things would get worse before they got better. As of 2010 the economy is showing signs of improving. There is the possibility of a new economy – a green economy with education as its lifeblood. One of the President's popular campaign proposals – a national infrastructure bank – is still on the agenda.

There is a movement toward clean air and a protected natural environment and the chance of improved foreign relations. President Obama received the Nobel Peace Prize in December 2009. Universal health care coverage is a reality. The public has been heard, and jobs are the primary issue at hand.

What is needed for the development of a rational economy is for the nation's educational system, especially in the fields of engineering, science, and math, to open the door to economic growth. A major result of past administrations has been joblessness and money in the hands of the few, but employment is picking up.

Americans as a nation of individuals want change. Democracy's founding principles of liberty, equality, and justice can be practiced ethically. We not only want change but can work to put it into effect. This depends not only on the government but upon each and all of us as individuals making our voices heard. We are each of us entitled to our own pursuit of happiness based upon self-love and the love of others.

Notes

Chapter One

[1] Edward Conrad Smith, ed., *The Constitution of the United States with Case Summaries* (New York: Barnes & Noble Books, 1972), 24.

[2] Ibid., 37.

[3] Alexis de Tocqueville, *Democracy in America*, Richard D. Heffner, ed. (New York: New American Library, 1959), 103.

Chapter 2

[1] Kathy L. Peiss, "American Woman and the Making of Modern Consumer Culture," The Journal for Multi Media History 1 (Aug. 24, 2006).

[2] Ibid., 1.

[3] Ibid., 2.

[4] John Kenneth Galbraith, *Economics and the Public Purpose* (Boston: Houghton Mifflin Co., 1973), 91.

[5] Ibid., 91.

[6] Erich Fromm, *The Sane Society* (New York: The New American Library, 1958), 175.

[7] Ibid., 175.

[8] James T. Patterson, *Restless Giant* (USA: Oxford University Press, 2005), 5.

[9] Ibid., 169.

[10] Ibid., 81.

[11] Ibid., 363.

[12] "One Day in America," *Time Magazine*, Nov. 26, 2007.

Chapter 3

[1] Martin Schram, *The Great American Video Game* (New York: William Morrow & Co., Inc., 1987), 15.

[2] Ibid., 25.

[3] Ibid., 56.

⁴ Samuel L. Popkin, "Changing Media, Changing Politics," *Perspectives on Politics* 4 (June 2006): 329.
⁵ Ibid., 329.
⁶ Ibid., 330.
⁷ Ibid., 333.
⁸ Ibid., 331.
⁹ Ibid., 333.

Chapter 4

¹ Peter Wollheim, "Anomie After Durkheim: Postmodernism and Suicide" (paper presented at international conference, Stockholm, Sweden, August 31, 2000) 3-4.
² Ibid., 4-5
³ Ibid., 5.
⁴ Alvin Toffler. *Third Wave, in Against the Machine* by Lee Siegel (New York: Spiegel & Grau, 2008), 58.
⁵ Ibid., 58
⁶ Ibid., 102.
⁷ Wollheim, "Anomie After Durkheim: Postmodernism and Suicide," 6.
⁸ Ibid., 8.
⁹ Siegel, *Against the Machine*, 21.
¹⁰ News report from NBC Nightly News with Brian Williams, New York: NBC World Headquarters, broadcast June 23, 2007.
¹¹ Siegel, *Against the Machine*, 157.
¹² Ibid., 157.
¹³ Ibid., 160.
¹⁴ Siegel, *Against the Machine*, 175.
¹⁵ Fromm, The Sane Society, 174.
¹⁶ Wollheim, "Anomie After Durkheim: Postmodernism and Suicide," 8.
¹⁷ Fromm, *The Sane Society*, 180-181.
¹⁸ Ibid., 180.
¹⁹ Frances Fox Piven, "Responses to American Democracy in an Age of Inequality," *PS: Political Science & Politics*. Online: http://www.apsanet.orgCambridge University Press, (January 2006),43.

Chapter 5

1. William B. Irvine, *On Desire* (Oxford, NY: Oxford University Press, 2006), 294.
2. A. de Tocqueville, *Democracy in America*, 144-145

Chapter 6

1. Robert Y. Shapiro, "The Meaning of American Democracy," *The Meaning of American Democracy*, ed. Robert Y. Shapiro (New York: The Academy of Political Science, 2005), 3.
2. Mortimer J. Adler, *Six Great Ideas* (New York: Macmillan Publishing Co., Inc., 1981), 168.
3. Smith, *The Constitution of the United States*, 24.
4. Mortimer Adler, *Six Great Ideas*, 169.
5. John Kenneth Galbraith, *The Affluent Society*, (New York: The New American Library, 1958), 242.
6. Robert Shapiro, *The Meaning of American Democracy*, 21.
7. Ibid., 20.
8. Ibid., 21.
9. Jerome Armstrong and Markos Moulitsas Zuniga, *Crashing the Gate: Netroots, Grassroots, and the Rise of People-Powered Politics* (Vermont: Chelsea Green Publishing Company, 2006), 176.
10. Ibid., 11.

Conclusion

1. Erich Fromm, *The Sane Society*, 179.
2. Erich Fromm, *To Have or To Be* (New York: Harper & Row, 1981), 155-157.
3. Paul Tillich, *The Courage to Be*, (New Haven: Yale University Press, 1967), 116.

Glossary

Alienation: A feeling that one's destiny is not under one's control. It causes one to feel estranged from the world, from one's work, and causes one to develop a sense of futility and powerlessness.

Anomie: A condition of rootlessness and normlessness; a condition of anxiety and amorality. It is caused by the absence of emotionally satisfying relationships. Individuals are forced into the weightless irrelevance of their personal affairs.

Anxiety: A state of undefined, unfocused fear.

Blogging: Consumer online self-expression.

Dialectic: The process of reasoning through the tension between opposing elements.

Ennui: Weariness and discontent resulting from having too much, from satiety.

"Mass man": A phrase denoting a male and a female in mass society.

Netroots: A term coined by Jerome Armstrong and Markos Moulitsas Zunigato in *Crashing the Gate* to describe online grassroots activity.

Post-modern man: The individual in today's high-tech world.

Sublimation: The process of projecting to a level of reality above the concrete present.

Synergy: synergism: The interaction of conditions such that the total effect is greater than the sum of the individual effects.

Resources

Books

Adler, Mortimer J. *Six Great Ideas*. New York: Macmillan Publishing Co., Inc., 1981 (theories on equality, justice, liberty and also truth, goodness, and beauty).

Almond, Gabriel A., and G. Bingham Powell, Jr. *Comparative Politics*. 2nd ed. Boston: Little, Brown and Company, 1965.

Armstrong, Jerome, and Markos Moulitsas Zuniga. *Crashing the Gate: Netroots, Grassroots, and the Rise of People-Powered Politics*. Vermont: Chelsea Green Publishing Company, 2006 (rise of political networking).

de Tocqueville, Alexis. *Democracy in America*. Edited by Richard D. Heffner, New York: New

American Library, 1959.

Dupré, Louis. *Transcendental Selfhood: The Rediscovery of the Inner Life*. New York: The Seabury Press, 1976.

Dupré, Louis. *Kierkegaard as Theologian: The Dialectic of Christian Existence*. New York: Sheed and Ward, 1963.

Fromm, Erich. *Escape from Freedom*. New York: A Discus Book published by Avon Books, 1965.

Fromm, Erich. *The Sane Society*. New York: Fawcett-World Library, 1969.

Fromm, Erich. *To Have or To Be?* New York: Harper & Row, 1981.

Fromm, Erich. *To Have or To Be?* New York: A Bantam New Age Book, 1982.

Galbraith, John Kenneth. *Economics and the Public Purpose*. Boston: Houghton Mifflin Co.,

1973.

Hall, Calvin S., and Vernon J. Norby. *A Primer of Jungian Psychology*. New York: A Mentor Book, 1973.

Irvine, William. *On Desire*. Oxford, NY: Oxford University Press, 2006.

Kaufman, Walter, ed. *Existentialism from Dostoevsky to Sartre*. New York: Plume-Penguin Group, 1975.

Jung, C.G. *Modern Man in Search of a Soul*. New York: Harcourt, Brace & World, Inc., 1933 (first-hand reading material by Jung).

Livingston, John C., and Robert G. Thompson. *The Consent of the Governed.* 2nd ed. New York: The Macmillan Company, 1966.

Mathews, David. *Politics for People,* 2nd ed. Chicago: University of Illinois Press, 1999.

Marcuse, Herbert. *One-Dimensional Man*. Boston: Beacon Press, 1968.

Muesing, Edith E. *The Alternative to Technological Culture*. NY: Colin-Press, 1986.

Muesing-Ellwood, Edith. *United States Democracy: Myth vs. Reality*. New York: Colin-Press, 1984.

Patterson, James T. *Restless Giant*. USA: Oxford University Press, 2005 (an excellent documentary on recent decades of social and political culture).

Riesman, David. *Abundance for What? And Other Essays*. New York: Doubleday & Co., Inc., 1964.

Schram, Martin. *The Great American Video Game*. New York: William Morrow & Co., Inc., 1987.

Shapiro, Robert, ed. *The Meaning of American Democracy*. New York: The Academy of Political Science, 2005.

Siegel, Lee. *Against the Machine*. New York: Spiegel & Grau, 2008 (interesting interpretation of computer culture).

Smith, Edward Conrad, ed. *The Cost of the US with Case Summaries*. New York: Barnes & Noble Books, 1972.

Tillich, Paul. *The Courage to Be*. New Haven: Yale University Press, 1967.

van der Post, Laurens. *Jung and the Story of Our Time*. New York: Pantheon Books, a division of Random House, 1975 (delves into C.G. Jung's life and his teachings)

Articles

Altman, Micah, and Kenneth Rogerson. "Open Research Questions on Information and Technology in Global and Domestic Politics–Beyond 'E.'" *Political Science and Politics* XLI (October 2008): 835-836.

Baker, Peter et al. "Administration is Seeking $700 Billion for Wall Street; Bailout Could Set Record. *New York Times*, September 21, 2008, 1, 30.

Best, Samuel J., et al. "The Polls-Trends: Privacy in the Information Age." *Public Opinion Quarterly* 70 (Fall 2006): 375-401.

Brettschneider, Cory. "The Politics of the Personal: A Liberal Approach." *American Political Science Review* 101 (February 2007): 27-30.

Caldwell, Christopher. "Not Being There." *The New York Times Magazine*, August 12, 2007, 11-12.

Craig, Susanne et al. "AIG, Lehman Shock Hits World Markets." *The Wall Street Journal*, September 16, 2008, A1-A2.

Daly, Herman E. "Entropy, Growth and the Political Economy of Scarcity." In *Scarcity and Growth Reconsidered*, edited by V. Kerry Smith. Baltimore: The Johns Hopkins University Press, 1982.

Farrier, Jasmine. "The Patriot Act's Institutional Story: More Evidence of Congressional Ambivalence." PS Online www.apsanet.org (January 2007) 83+.

Frank, Thomas. Excerpt from *Conquest of Cool: Business Culture, Counterculture, and the Rise of Hip Consumerism* (Chicago: University of Chicago Press, 1997), http://www.press.uchicago.edu/Misc/Chicago/259919.html.

"gen M." *Time Magazine*, March 27, 2006.

Gibbs, Nancy. "One Day in America." *Time Magazine*, November 26, 2007, 36+.

"Homo Mobilis." *The Economist* (April 12, 2008): 17-18.

"In 2008, Be Nicer to Your Neighbors." *The World in 2008 – The Economist*. http://www.economist.com/theWorldIn/china/displayStory.cfm?story_id=10125673&d=2008.

Kluth, Andreas. "Nomads at Last." *The Economist* (April 12, 2008): 3-5.

Ibid., 3-18.

"Labour Movement." *The Economist* (April 12, 2008): 5-8.

Mazzeti, Mark. "Spy Agencies." *New York Times*, September 24, 2006, 8.

McCann, James A., and David P. Redlawsk. "As Voters Head to the Polls, Will They Perceive a 'Culture of Corruption.'" *Political Science and Politics* XXXIX (October 2006): 797-802.

Milkis, Sidney M. and Jesse H. Rhodes. "George W. Bush, the Republican Party, and the 'New' American Party System." *Perspectives on Politics* 5 (September 2007): 461-488.

Morgenson, Gretchen. "Given a Shovel, Digging Deeper Into Debt." *New York Times*, July 20, 2008, 1, 14.

Owen, J. Judd. "The Struggle between 'Religion and Nonreligion.': Jefferson, Backus, and Dissonance of America's Founding Principles. *American Political Science Review* 101 (August 2007): 493-504.

Peiss, Kathy L. "American Women and the Making of Modern Consumer Culture." *The Journal for MultiMedia History* 1 (August 24, 2006): 1-9.

Pinker, Steven. "The Mystery of Consciousness." *Time Magazine*, January 29, 2007, 61.

Piven, Frances Fox. "Response to American Democracy in an Age of Inequality." PS Online. PS: Political Science & Politics, www.apsnet.org, vol. 39, issue 01. Cambridge University Press (January 2006): 43-57.

Popkin, Samuel L. "Changing Media, Changing Politics." *Perspectives on Politics* 4 (June 2006): 327-341 (excellent article on media and politics today).

Slater, Jerome. "Tragic Choices in the War on Terrorism: Should We Try to Regulate and Control Torture?" *Political Science Quarterly* 121 (Summer 2006): 191-202.

Stengel, Richard. "The New Patriotism." *Time Magazine*, July 7, 2008, 25.

"Stimulus and Shopping." *The Economist* (May 31, 2008): 34.

Wollheim, Peter. "Anomie After Durkheim: Postmodernism and Suicide." Paper presented at international conference, Stockholm, Sweden, August 31, 2000, 1-11.

Reports

James A. Baker III, et al. *The Iraq Study Group Report*. New York: Vintage Books, a division of Random House, Inc., 2006.

Media

NBC Nightly News with Brian Williams. New York: NBC World Headquarters. June 23, 2007, broadcast 6:30 p.m.

Internet Listing

"Making the Technologies Work for Us," 1-4. http://www/netaction.org/bollier/part2c.htm

Ross, Kristina. "Mass Culture." http://www.mediahistory.umn.edu/masscult.html(accessed August 31, 2006).

"The Computer Culture." http://www.units.muohio.edu//englishtech/eng49501/moscakj/essay.htm (accessed September 1, 2006)

Edith E. Muesing-Ellwood

Additional Works

Books

Dodd, Lawrence C., and Bruce I. Oppenheimer. *Congress Reconsidered.* Washington, D.C.: CQPress, 2001.

Fromm, Erich. *Man for Himself.* New York: Fawcett Premier, 1975.

Sargent, S. Stanfeld, and Kenneth R. Stafford. *Basic Techniques of the Great Psychologists.*

Garden City, New York: Doubleday & Company, Inc., 1965.

Vaughn, Karen Iversen. *John Locke: Economist and Social Scientist.* Chicago: The University of Chicago Press, 1982.

Articles

Brettschneider, Corey. "The Politics of the Personal: A Liberal Approach." *American Political Science Review* 101 (February 2007): 19-31.

Caldwell, Christopher. "Not Being There." *The New York Times Magazine*, August 12, 2007, 11, 12.

Coles, Romand. "Of Tensions and Tricksters: Grassroots Democracy between Theory and

Practice. *Perspectives on Politics* 4 (September 2006): 547-559.

———. "Futurists Mark New Year with 10 Forecasts." *Engineering Times.* (January 1987): 11+.

Henig, Robin Marantz. "God has always been a puzzle." *The New York Times Magazine*, March 4, 2007, 38-43+

Kleinerman, Benjamin. "Can the Prince Really Be Tamed? Executive Prerogative, Popular

 Apathy and the Constitutional Frame in Locke's Second Treatises." *American Political Science Review* 101 (May 2007): 209-222.

Miller, Lisa L. "The Representational Biases of Federalism: Scope and Bias in the Political Process, Revisited." *Perspectives on Politics* 5 (June 2007): 305-321.

Internet Listings

Carson, Stephen. "The Rise of Producer Culture," (September 3, 2006): 1-4, ttp://openfiction.blogspot.com/2005/08/rise-of-producer-culture.html.

⎯⎯⎯⎯⎯⎯⎯. "Creating a Telecommunications Architecture That Supports Community, Democracy and Culture," (September 7, 2006): 1-3, http://www/netaction.org/bollier/part1c.htm.

"The Future Is Already Here, It's Just Unevenly Distributed," (September 3, 2006): 11-14 http://wwwtedfriedman.com/.

Irvine, Dr. Ian. "Towards an Outline of Postmodern Ennui." *The Antigonish Review* 116

(September 20, 2006): 1-19, http://www.antigonishreview.com/bi-116/116-irvine.html.

Jihad – Wikipedia, the free encyclopedia. thtp://en.wikipedia.org/wiki/Jihad (accessed June 29, 2006).

Weiss, Dennis M. "Human Nature and the Digital Culture: The Case for Philosophical Anthropology," (September 1, 2006), http://www.bu.edu/wcp/Papers/Anth/AnthWeis.htm.

About the Author

Edith E. Muesing-Ellwood is a freelance writer with a background in political science. She earned her Bachelor's degree from Fordham University and her Master's degree from New York University. She later studied at the Graduate School of East Stroudsburg University in Pennsylvania. She was the recipient of a four-year New York State Regents Scholarship, a graduate research assistantship, and a graduate work-study grant.

Edith is the author of the books *The Alternative To Technological Culture* and *United States Democracy: Myth Vs. Reality*. Her essays, articles, and short stories have appeared in such journals as *The St. Croix Review*, *The Black Mountain Review*, *Expressions Magazine*, and *Both Sides Now*.

Her honors include the distribution of a seminar paper, "Technological Culture, Ethics, and Religion," by the Society for Philosophy and Technology in Enschede, The Netherlands in 1985 and Editor's Choice Award For Outstanding Achievement in Poetry presented by poetry.com and the International Library of Poetry in March 2005.

Edith is a member of the American Political Science Association, the Academy of Political Science, the Wilson Center Associates, the National Writers Union, the International Women's Writing Guild, the Sierra Club, and the Democratic National Committee.

She is currently researching an article on women in Afghanistan today, writes haiku, and edits research on a voluntary basis. She lives with her husband, Danny Ellwood, in the Pocono Mountains and has three adult children.

www.ingramcontent.com/pod-product-compliance
Lightning Source LLC
Chambersburg PA
CBHW070031040426
42333CB00040B/1535